THE MAKING OF

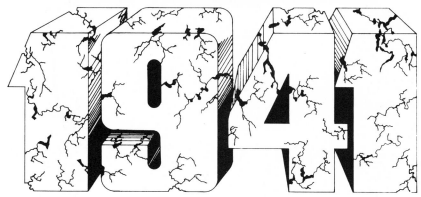

250

THE MAKING OF

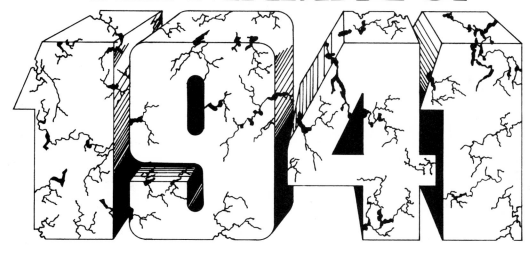

Glenn Erickson
and
Mary Ellen Trainor

BALLANTINE BOOKS · NEW YORK

Library of Congress Catalog Card Number: 79-92298

ISBN 0-345-28924-2

Manufactured in the United States of America

First Edition: February 1980

CONTENTS

AUTHORS' NOTE

Steven Spielberg believes that *1941* is only a BIG movie if you sit in the front row of the theater. We think the information contained in the following pages contradicts that statement.

1941 is an epic motion picture. To transform the comedy spectacular from the written page to the screen was a tremendous task. But, despite overwhelming odds it was a labor of love for all those who combined their talents on behalf of the project.

We only hope you enjoy seeing *1941* as much as we enjoyed making it.

Chapter One

THE BIRTH OF A GIANT

1941 began in 1975. As with most creative endeavors, whether designing an electrically powered automobile or developing a motion picture, the nurturing process is a long one.

Robert Zemeckis and Bob Gale were two aspiring film writers, as well as World War II buffs. At one point in their research, they found mention of a particularly odd event that occurred in the early days of the Second World War. The coast of Santa Barbara was torpedoed by a Japanese submarine in February 1942, resulting in a mistaken Japanese air raid on the city of Los Angeles! Hysteria and panic gripped residents from Southern California to Oregon. For the war-nervous citizenry it was an unnatural occurrence. For Zemeckis and Gale it was a natural. They took the idea to writer/director John Milius. An avid war historian himself, Milius was easily convinced. He commissioned the two to write a movie based on the incident and its aftermath.

The first draft of the screenplay was completed in May of 1975; only a month had passed since the discovery of the event. The facts had been remarkably embellished and little in the story remained historically accurate. With Milius, the writers went further and laced the screenplay with pure outrageousness. Later, when filmmaker Steven Spielberg joined in their idea sessions, the project was described as approaching a "critical mass" intensity.

Steven Spielberg, the dynamic director whose blockbuster hits included *Jaws* and *Close Encounters of the Third Kind,* committed himself to the project in 1976. He had been introduced to the concept a year earlier by John Milius, and he loved it! "It was a great moment of glory reading the script and deciding to make the movie," Spielberg said. "I didn't consider *1941* an out-and-out comedy so much as a colossal action adventure. Comedy was the byproduct of foolishness, panic, and paranoia. Paranoia sometimes being my middle name, I decided this was a movie I could do better than perhaps an *Annie Hall* or *Divorce Italian Style.*"

In July of 1976, Spielberg summoned Zemeckis and Gale to Alabama, where he was filming *Close Encounters of the Third Kind.* For nearly two months the three labored over the script and took further license with the original concept. They molded a narrative involving the exploits of a Japanese submarine crew and a middle-class American family. The story would take place within a twenty-four-hour period six days after the attack on Pearl Harbor in December 1941.

"I'm just like any other member of a theater audience," said Spielberg. "I like to choke on my popcorn when something really funny happens. I felt *1941* was the kind of picture I'd pay to go see if someone else were to make it. So why not beat that someone else to it and make it myself?"

Nearly five years, nine screenplay drafts, nine hundred employees, two hundred and forty-seven shooting days, and 658,650 feet of film later, the largest comedy misadventure in movie-making history was born.

Spielberg wanted to give *1941* the look and feel of the movies of that period. Rather than use the sophisticated shooting system in which camera moves are actually computerized, he chose the proven special effects processes used in the great war movies. He improved upon them by marrying the older techniques with the newer processes using optical effects.

Making all of *1941* work would tax even Einstein. How could two World War II aircraft strafe one another over Hollywood Boulevard? How could an entire amusement park be blown up by a Japanese submarine lurking off the California coast? It could only be done by the magic of Hollywood—and then some.

"A key element in a movie the size of *1941* is to surround yourself with the best people in the business," Spielberg theorized. "A movie as complicated as *'41* could not be made without mustering the greatest conceivable army of expert craftspeople. I was fortunate such individuals were available to help me."

A core group of these masters was assembled in the autumn of 1977. Greg Jein, genius modelmaker who was responsible for the Mothership miniature in *Close Encounters,* made a smooth transition to *1941.* A. D. Flowers, one of the

Steven Spielberg

Spielberg with Director of Photography Bill Fraker

premiere explosive and complicated mechanical effects men in the industry, was wooed out of retirement by Spielberg. *1941* promised to be a heavy explosion show with numerous mechanical rigs to be constructed. A. D. also had years of experience under his belt in rigging miniatures. William (Bill) Fraker, the Academy Award-nominated cinematographer, was drafted while working with Spielberg on *Close Encounters.* He thrived on challenges like *1941.* Terry Leonard was hired as *'41*'s stunt coordinator shortly after his employment on *Apocalypse Now* in the Philippines. For those of us who often trip over our own two feet, the thought of responsibly coordinating the movements of over six hundred men involved in a riot was enough to bring us to our knees! Production illustrator George Jensen had the job of putting Spielberg's vision of the movie on paper. He eventually produced over four

Film editor Michael Kahn (l.) with 1941 *authors Robert Zemeckis and Bob Gale*

hundred drawings that were continually referred to during the filming. Once a particular scene sketch was completed, it was up to production designer Dean Mitzner to give it life.

Steven Spielberg's imagination was overwhelming; and for eighteen months these individuals and scores more combined their talents to transpose the script to the screen.

Where was such a crew to be housed? Proximity to one another was crucial for the exchange of facts and ideas. Scores of props were used in 1941—where were they to be safely kept? Miniatures the size of city blocks needed to be built. In addition, it was possible that filming of the miniature sets might have to be done in the same location. Where could a location be found that met all of these specifications?

The hunt was an exasperating one. Finally, the production company found itself at the door of a vacant Lockheed airplane hangar in Burbank, California. The hangar was damp, cold, noisy, BIG, and perfect.

By the autumn of 1977 preproduction was well under way. The hangar was home base for nearly every facet of the movie. With each week that passed, producer Buzz Feitshans added to the growing ranks of technicians and consultants. Production meetings were held on a weekly basis. Crammed into a hastily built room in a corner of the hangar, key personnel discussed every detail of the movie with Spielberg.

During the early stages it was obvious that the nature of the beast was accelerated growth. If you go to the grocery store without a list, most likely you will walk every aisle and eventually spend more money than you originally intended to. The making of a movie is very similar. The policing of every dollar falls on the shoulders of the producer. Buzz Feitshans clearly stated the economic philosophy of 1941: "It's not whether you use computers or Scotch tape; what matters is the result." Feitshans was to watch more than twenty-six million dollars leave the kitty.

Over one million dollars of that figure was consumed by the cast of 1941. The script contained sixty-five speaking roles. Each part demanded special attention by both Spielberg and his casting director, Sally Dennison. Casting a movie of this magnitude was a tremendous chore of compiling pictures, resumes, and tapes. '41 had twenty leading characters—an uncommonly high number.

A director, despite input from all sources, is ultimately responsible for the casting of the film. Spielberg was no exception. Actors and actresses filed into Spielberg's office every thirty minutes from nine in the morning until eight at night.

Already at the top of his mental cast list were John Belushi and Dan Aykroyd. These two young men had been catapulted to stardom through their weekly appearances on NBC's Saturday Night Live. They were the heroes of America's youth; Spielberg wanted them as the heroes of his comedy spectacular. Despite scheduling difficulties, Belushi was signed to play the crazed pilot, Wild Bill Kelso. Aykroyd, who would be making his feature film debut, would play the tank commander, Sergeant Tree. Throughout the filming of 1941 the production schedule was shuffled time and time again to accommodate their weekly television appearances. Only when the show was on

John Belushi

hiatus for the season were Belushi and Aykroyd available to the movie company for more than two days a week.

As time went on, Spielberg secured the actor of his choice of every role in the film. Advertisements for the movie would eventually boast of a cast of some of Hollywood's finest actors. Ned Beatty was cast as the patriotic American defending his home against being shelled by a Japanese submarine; Lorraine Gary, as his confused and courageous wife; Robert Stack, as the heralded

Dan Aykroyd

Lorraine Gary, Ned Beatty and family

Robert Stack

Warren Oates

THE MAKING OF 1941

General Stilwell; Warren Oates, as the paranoid Army colonel holed up in the desert; Christopher Lee, as the misplaced German officer; Murray Hamilton, as the stranded civil defense volunteer; Slim Pickens, as the foolhearty farmer taken hostage by the Japanese; Lionel Stander, who protects himself against the enemy by converting his car into a tank; and Tim Matheson and Treat Williams as the young soldiers fighting for the right to the women of their dreams.

Christopher Lee

Slim Pickens

Tim Matheson

Treat Williams

The Birth of a Giant

Toshiro Mifune

When it was announced that the celebrated Japanese actor Toshiro Mifune would play the commander of a Japanese submarine, suspicion arose of divine powers at work on *1941.* It was an honor to have him for the role of Commander Mitamura.

Video audition tapes were the catalysts for much of the remaining casting. In the case of Bobby Di Cicco, whose only previous feature credit was *I Wanna Hold Your Hand,* reading before the camera meant victory. He won the coveted role of Wally, a lovesick teenager who, declared unfit for military duty, puts his war effort into winning a jitterbug contest!

Dianne Kay and Bobby Di Cicco

THE MAKING OF 1941

With the additions of Nancy Allen as a secretary enamored of military aircraft, Dianne Kay as the naive USO hostess sought after by every man in uniform, Wendie Jo Sperber as her energetic and adventurous girlfriend, and, finally, Eddie Deezen as the mischievous war volunteer stuck atop a Ferris wheel, the casting was complete.

Nancy Allen

ine Kay

Wendie Jo Sperber

The Birth of a Giant

The assemblage was one of professionals committed to their art. Spielberg worked closely with each actor to help fully develop his or her character. During the long months of shooting they demanded a lot of one another: for example, on particular sets Spielberg would insist that every actor be present whether written into the scene or not. If he had an idea that involved a character, the actor had to be available at a moment's notice. But Steven Spielberg's direction and relationships with his actors put to rest any doubt that he was not an actor's director. Commented Robert Stack: "Spielberg really likes actors without indulging them, and the actor senses it immediately. Like Kazan with Brando, he would find keys that opened the door to a good performance. Spielberg cannot part the Red Sea, but he can make an actor better. For me, he made *1941* an unequaled joy. It was like recess in kindergarten."

Robert Stack as General Stilwell reads Life Magazine *with the real General Stilwell on the cover*

Chapter Two

A SMALL WORLD

Much of what was in the script of *1941* was literally larger than life. It could not possibly be shot entirely on real locations with real people. If you cannot blow up the local amusement park, there is only one alternative: build it so that you can. But rather than build it according to authentic dimensions, fashion it to be not much larger than a tabletop erector set. Camera tricks do the rest.

1941 called for five full sets to be manufactured in miniature. A dimension of one and one-half inches to the foot was chosen as a workable scale.

The extensive period research on *1941* reached into every facet of the film. Work on the Ocean Pier Park miniature began the first day that drawings from the art department were delivered—a total of one hundred and forty-four sketches pertained to this set alone. As many as seven or eight constituted a single structure that would inevitably be struck and demolished by a Japanese torpedo. The scope of the project prompted model supervisor Greg Jein to

divide his labor force into teams with specialized functions. Some of the more detailed buildings were assigned to individual propmakers. "Toonerville," for instance, a crooked haunted house based on a legendary '40's park exhibit, did not contain a single straight line in its blueprints. Every miniature edifice was painted with skill and imagination. External details of rough stucco and uneven plaster were added. All of these creations—which could be held in the palm of a hand—were further aged with an oil and thinner wash that dulled the bright colors on penny arcades and snack emporiums. The look of peeling paint was achieved with additives that caused the pigments to shrink and crack as they dried. Spielberg's rule of thumb was "dull it down, dirty it up, rust it over." Sparkling amusement parks did not exist.

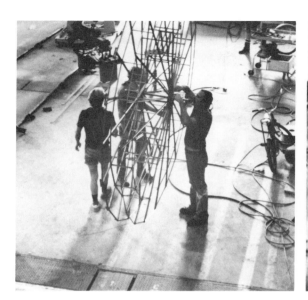

Director Spielberg was obsessed with detail. Every door had a hinge and every window had a frame. The intricate structures had interior lights and displayed rows of colored bulbs on their facades. The lights for the miniatures became their most expensive and consuming decor. Two thousand bulbs were wired into a Ferris wheel alone. Aside from this spectacular wheel, which would eventually dislodge itself and roll down the park's pier to a watery death, there were a roller coaster, a merry-go-round, a tunnel of love, hot dog concessions, popcorn stands, and more. The only disappointment was that those who labored so long and hard would never experience the thrill of a ride or the misery of indigestion from too much cotton candy. It was a small fantasy ... a toy that every child dreamed of.

For scale, see technician's body at far right

Miniature Ferris wheel with anima-
tronic figures

    Miniature people also had to be designed to work within the Ocean Park sequence. Two civil defense volunteers, played by Murray Hamilton and Eddie Deezen, are involuntarily marooned atop the Ferris wheel while keeping watch for enemy forces. The enemy force is a Japanese submarine positioned frightfully close to the amusement park. The sub crew includes characters played by Toshiro Mifune and Christopher Lee. Disney technician Robert Johnston built the animatronic figures after much experimentation. The dolls used were action figures of the GI Joe type. At the one-and-one-half-inch scale, the park was less than Barbie Doll size. Spielberg settled for radio control of the figures after numerous tests were made of different methods. The dolls' transmitter-actuators were hidden along with their batteries wherever possible. Off in the wings was propmaker Ken Swenson, who controlled their movements. Tiny costumes were fashioned to match the wardrobe of their real-life counterparts. Because the story called for Eddie Deezen to have a

Close-up of the animatronic dolls

ventriloquist's dummy in his likeness as a constant companion, a figurine as big as a paper clip was designed to resemble his hand puppet. Seen from only a few feet away, the tiny dolls were totally convincing.

A. D. Flowers was ready to test some of the bigger special effects demanded in *1941*. The process was begun very early in the preproduction phase to allow ample time for perfecting. Tests of every kind became imperative in the overall filmmaking process. Disaster strikes when a full shooting day is in swing and an effect fails. An actor can be reminded of his lines without costing money. But failure of a mechanical effect or a physical stunt can cost thousands of dollars when filming is halted for corrective measures. Spielberg never wanted a particular set to supersede a gag. Each one had to be magnificent and, more often than not, hysterically funny. "A sight gag or a special effect within a comedy spectacular like *'41* isn't worth the powder it's kindled with unless it gets a laugh, unless the audience likes it," remarked Spielberg. "It might take two weeks to create and perform a complicated physical sight gag, but if the audience doesn't howl, that's two weeks on the cutting-room floor."

One test that proved funny by itself involved a full-sized torpedo. A scene, eventually cut from the script, called for a Japanese torpedo to jump from the water and chase one of the characters through many of the amusement park's attractions. The test took place at the hangar, where eighty feet of track was laid along one wall. Two roller-skate-like wheel assemblies were welded on either end of the steel torpedo replica. These wheels would roll the torpedo through the track. To power the bullet-shaped projectile, effects man Terry Frazee connected cable from the nose to a jeep. Acceleration! Action! The torpedo flew smoothly down the rails. Success! Frazee hit the brakes and the cable unexpectedly snapped. The torpedo shot off the track, ran across the floor, and smashed through the corrugated steel hangar wall at forty miles an hour.

Other effects tests proved remarkably innovative. Because a World War II Warhawk airplane, piloted by John Belushi, was to fly through the amusement park, a miniature model aircraft was required. Getting it to fly at the director's

Executive Producer John Milius and Producer Buzz Feitshans examine the unusual damage

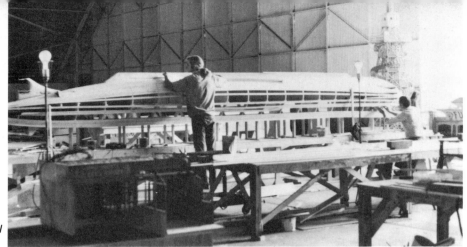

Propmakers fashion the hull of the 27-foot model submarine

command was also up to A. D. Flowers. The solution was to erect guillotines at both ends of the stage. Wires were connected to the balsa wood wings (wingspan being fifty-seven inches compared to the full-sized thirty-eight feet). Initially the plane was radio-controlled, but failed to stop without tremendous impact. Manpower was chosen as the next best tool. Cables connected to the guillotine wires were pulled by hand to give the little model speed up to forty miles per hour.

Searchlights over the city of Los Angeles presented an awkward problem. They had to be seen crisscrossing the sky behind Ocean Pier Park. First, lasers created by mirrors and lenses were split into a dozen miniature beams. From behind cardboard cutouts that gave the illusion of mountains, they beamed broad shafts of brilliant white light up to the rafters, so bright they were not believable. Optical consultant Bill Abbott, a master at getting the camera to perform miracles, had an ingenious idea: Scotchlite material was affixed to single slats of thin lumber. A small spotlight was positioned alongside the camera, aimed at the highly reflective strips. The result was the precise glow given off by an authentic searchlight. A total of twenty-four of these wigwagging beams, each twenty feet long and controlled by an electric motor, eventually functioned in the sky over Los Angeles.

Tampering with natural forces was a special challenge to the effects crew. If a miniature submarine was to waiver off Ocean Park's pier, it could not very well be photographed in the Pacific Ocean. The waves would be triple its size. Twenty-seven feet was the entire length of the small vessel. It was constructed with a precision equaling a real I-boat. A keel was laid and a series of bulkheads attached. Thin wooden strips were then tacked on, giving shape to the structure. Jacketed in heat-forming plastic foam, the submarine then received a final covering of fiberglass. Plastic tubing became torpedo tubes.

The 27-foot sub in its final phase of construction

The rudder was aluminum-reinforced, and diving planes and stabilizer fins were made to withstand rough treatment and, most importantly, to survive the thrashing tides. Producing miniature waves was another challenge tackled by the crew. Several wet-suit-clad crew members stood waist-deep in chilling waters to stir the sea. They created swells by pushing down on large planks of wood at regular intervals. The submarine rocked back and forth at a believable pace. Small agitation machines and ritter fans also contributed to the desired effect.

Steven Spielberg and his director of photography, Bill Fraker, shot tests over and over again until the effects were perfect. Both were relentlessly detail-oriented—not a single storyboard drawing went by without their determining the feasibility of its content. Spielberg and Fraker had developed a warm and tenacious relationship: Fraker, blessed with a wonderful sense of humor, was often the comic relief for the director and the entire crew.

A Small World

Rigging the pier to explode

On October 23, 1978, photography on *1941* officially began. A cake-and-champagne toast to the wizardry of Greg Jein and his crew christened the shooting.

Stage 30 on the Metro-Goldwyn-Mayer studio lot had never looked so breathtaking. This particular location had been built in the early 1950's and had the largest indoor water tank in all of Los Angeles. Measuring ninety by one hundred and ten feet, the swimming pool had been designed for screen star Esther Williams. Now it was transformed into the Pacific Ocean! At the opposite end of the stage a huge wooden platform acted as the foundation for Ocean Pier Park. Elaborate modifications were made in the stage rafters to accommodate the complicated lighting system needed to illuminate the miniature; every camera move altered the lighting scheme. Sand and rock for the long, wide beach were laid, having arrived in an endless procession of trucks and bins. Extending from the same to the water stood Ocean Park's giant pier. Required to support a careening Ferris wheel, it was fifty-one feet long and thirteen feet high. Its entire underbelly was laced with primacord explosives. Hanging lights lit both sides of the pier, and fancy pillar lamps were positioned along the boardwalk. The beautifully detailed carnival of rides and buildings were placed on the platform. Many of them, shaped from balsa wood to explode easily, were re-situated over and over until the exact submarine shelling hits were determined. When everything was finally anchored, a hole was cut in the platform under each structure to allow access to the miniature set lights inside. Hundreds of circuits had to be routed between the buildings and the master control panels situated at the rear of the park. Hours of labor were logged below the plant in a claustrophobic maze of wood, wires, and pipes. Hundreds of petite string lights crisscrossed the arcade. Tiny pieces of furniture, gumball machines, bicycles in racks, prizes for the game booths, and

Production Illustrator George Jensen's sketch of the Ferris wheel leaving its mooring

newspaper stands whose papers screamed "WAR" in bite-sized print graced the entire set. Every period-perfect item was minute enough to swallow. Like Alice's falling down the rabbit hole, it was an unforgettable trip through Wonderland.

A major equipment problem was gratefully avoided in the early stages of preproduction. The motion-picture camera, with its variety of hardware and movement apparatus, is a very cumbersome piece of machinery, that could not possibly be maneuvered within the miniature to capture the action on film. An innovative new camera, developed by two Frenchmen and never before used in the United States, caught Spielberg's attention. The Louma, as it is called, is a remote-controlled video camera suspended at the end of a long steel arm. An operator sits at a console and controls the camera's movement with geared head wheels, while a television monitor shows him what the camera sees. With the ability to rotate an entire 360 degrees, the control elements could be well removed from what was being shot. Thus, the Louma camera could find its way into the smallest corners of the fragile miniature while the operator remained safely at a distance. Many of the intricate shots Spielberg achieved would not have been possible without it.

The fog rolls in ...

Filming the action at Ocean Pier Park was a genuine thrill. Cameraman Fraker gave the deserted, oceanside replica a fog-shrouded appearance. Several times a day a fog machine filled the stage with thick, oily smoke. A dangerous piece of special effects equipment, it is used by Navy vessels to generate smoke screens.

Although it was sad to witness such resplendent work dissolving in ruin, the excitement of the explosions was undeniable. "Emulsify it," Spielberg repeated until the countdown was complete. One by one, the architectural masterpieces fell victim to the imaginary torpedo hits. Fountains of debris shot into the air, windows and doors blew out, walls of breakaway glass exploded into the arcade streets. It was a stunningly choreographed ballet of destruction.

Three different explosive effects were used. Flowers employed powder to break apart structures, air mortars to blow debris into the air, and flashbulbs from an everyday pocket camera to provide sporadic flashes of light. These bulbs were coated with flash powder to render airplane flak bursts in the sky. For each take sometimes up to fifty bulbs had to be hurriedly replaced by hand! Rigging even the smallest of blasts summoned every ounce of expertise A. D. Flowers and his men could muster.

Sketch of the park as shelling commences

"The Ferris wheel in *1941* is my 'Mothership.' It is the one effect that must be a one hundred per cent unqualified knockout," Spielberg directed. And it was. The wheel, a twenty-sided polygon, measured eleven feet in diameter and tipped the scales at one hundred and sixty pounds. Out of control, it had to whirl down the park's pier and catapult into the sea. Spielberg wanted repeatable, controllable sixty-foot sprints, but securing such an extraordinary effect posed dozens of dilemmas.

First, a catwalk was riveted to the rafters of the stage. Fastened to it was an "upside down" track on which a motorized cart ran, with the Ferris wheel suspended below it on four cables. Hanging in that position, the magnificently

A Small World

lit circle was spun by hand. The cables were then cut and, still attached to the rails, the wheel would revolve down the pier at high speed, giving it the semblance of rolling across the pier planks and tearing them apart. In actuality, the wheel hovered just above the pier, and the detonation of buried charges would blast it to kindling.

"Action! Fire the charges! Roll the wheel!" The command echoed through the stage and pierced the ears of excited spectators. Pyrotechnics shot off under the wheel, effects men pulled the cables, and a string of rapid gunshots tore at the wheel's base. The giant, glittering amusement ride spun wildly down the pier until it plunged into the waters below and sank like a stone! It looked like a tremendous jewel loosened from its setting. Seven cameras captured the spectacle from every angle.

There had been larger miniatures before Ocean Pier Park, but never one as detailed. It was the most ambitious ever built for a motion picture. For only a few minutes on screen, it had cost over one million dollars to create. And it was reduced to rubble with hardly a souvenir remaining.

28

Chapter Three

THE REAL THING

The transition from the land of make-believe to reality was a smooth one. No one had enough time even to think about it. All during the miniature photography, preparations for principal shooting were made. Frequent production meetings were held, actors had extensive rehearsals, locations were secured and sets built.

More reams of research on the 1940's were compiled. Every department—wardrobe, hair, props, transportation—utilized research houses, magazines, libraries, grandparents, and county records.

At one point, Spielberg called attention to the set dressing in an Army barracks location. "There weren't any beer cans in 1941. Somebody goofed."

Property master Sammy Gordon's quick-witted response was to produce a 1939 newspaper ad, depicting Pabst Blue Ribbon Beer in cans. It was hard to catch the forty-year veteran napping.

One of 1941's largest undertakings was to secure authentic military memorabilia. Spielberg had done his homework, and he refused to be compromised until all possibilities were exhausted. Necessary props ranged from automatic weapons to tanks and airplanes. The United States Army chose not to cooperate with the film company, refusing to donate or sell any battle specimens. It found one of 1941's main characters—the trigger-happy, misdirected World War II pilot, portrayed by John Belushi—to be especially unappealing. So, a countrywide search was initiated to procure an inventory of military weapons and vehicles.

Most difficult to obtain was a General Lee M3 medium tank. Such tanks were as rare as gold bullion. Most of them had been given to the United States allies when the less vulnerable Sherman tank came into being. Spielberg would accept no alternates, but he had no choice in this: a World War II Priest tank was converted into an M3. The basic chassis was nearly identical to the Lee, and a turret and hatch fashioned from balsa wood and scrap metal made it authentic.

Other hardware, including cannons, antiaircraft guns, and airplanes, came from museums across the country. Transporting them to the Burbank hangar and to each location was a delicate and expensive job.

The Indian Dunes Desert was the first location for 1941. It was transformed into Army barracks to house the deranged Madman Maddox, portrayed by Warren Oates. Set decorators scattered clusters of sandbag bunkers with camouflage netting, while stacks of shells, boxes of ammunition, and rows of

Construction of the smallest tank miniature

The actual-size tank, christened "Lulubelle"

Propmakers work to "age" the aircraft

Madman Maddox on alert

31

bombs were everywhere. Shooting was done at night and in nearly freezing temperatures. Rain pelted the crew for days. Hollywood can start fake rain on cue but cannot stop the real thing!

Extras were given lessons in how to hold and fire authentic World War II Thompson submachine guns, in the first of many scenes that called for military weaponry. Stembridge Guns, a rental facility, supplied the film with over two hundred guns. The "soldiers" of *1941* fired fifty thousand rounds of ammunition before the movie was over. (Many of those same weapons had actually been borrowed to defend the California coast during World War II.)

Scenes shot at Indian Dunes contained complicated special effects and difficult physical stunts. Both A. D. Flowers and Terry Leonard had their hands full. Writers Zemeckis and Gale were now on the set—along with Spielberg, the two writers would retire to the warmth of a motor home in between camera

setups. After bouncing story ideas back and forth, the three eventually emerged with wilder notions and "greater inspirations." More often than not, the crew paled at the director's new concepts, for they were rarely less than near-impossible.

The night of the biggest stunt was a particularly cold and damp one. Action entailed a Beechcraft trainer taxiing down a makeshift runway, catching a wing tip, and thrashing a twenty-five-foot spotting tower to the mud. Construction coordinator Mickey Woods built the breakaway tower to carefully drafted specifications. The effects crew rigged the tower's key supports to collapse when it was struck by the airplane; but if the wing tip actually hit the structure, the plane could very well spin out of control. Consequently, on cue, the tower would snap and crumble just as the wing tip passed. Stacks of cardboard boxes were piled in pits dug to soften the landing of two stuntmen. Perched atop the tower, they were costumed as enemy aircraft spotters.

After hours of preparation, the accumulated tension was released in a few violent, noisy seconds. The aircraft lumbered by the tower, stuntmen leaped from their perch, and the tower succumbed gracefully when its hidden cables were released. All cameras caught the action—including one buried beneath the tower inches from splintered lumber. There was only one casualty: a rubber rifle worn by stunt coordinator Leonard was bent in the shape of a half-moon!

"Look at what you did to my rifle," lamented property master Gordon.

"Better it than me, babe," answered Leonard.

A special excitement filled the air at Indian Dunes when John Belushi began work on *1941.* Whenever shooting was delayed, the crew took advantage of lapses in the action to request autographs. Performing as Wild Bill Kelso, Belushi was totally enthralling; he moved confidently into the role and filled it

34

Wild Bill Kelso's P-40 Warhawk

with his own manic energy. Comrade and fellow *'41* star Danny Aykroyd
shared Belushi's enthusiasm. Their fervor was contagious.

During filming, both frequently sought refuge in their trailers and in the
company of a few close friends. Once their first album, "The Blues Brothers,"
hit the top of the charts, they became stars—and found that privacy could not
be bought.

Despite the opportunities for injury, *1941* was completed with an almost
clean bill of health. One of the few mishaps involved John Belushi. A scene in
the desert dictated that he make a running dash for his P-40 Warhawk airplane,
jump up on the wing, and drop himself into the cockpit. Too much momentum
caused John to lose his balance on the wing. Headfirst, he fell seven feet to the
crusty earth. Rumors of his death were greatly exaggerated. Belushi did
survive, and the accident was later cut into the movie.

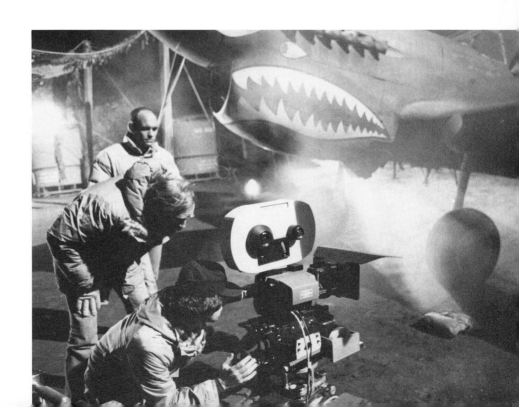

"Gas Mama" Lucille Bensen approaches the plane

Belushi was already famous for his "food-fight" scene in *Animal House,* and the *1941* script called for Wild Bill Kelso to go on a binge through a desert cafe. A rundown gas station and neighboring cafe were dressed to serve as Wild Bill's refueling stop. Situated in the desert of Aqua Dulce, the location had been used by Spielberg in his critically acclaimed movie *Duel.*

Location manager Tony Brown had to secure a number of permits for the site, particularly for the use of pyrotechnics. In one scene, the entire gas island erupted in a tremendous fireball and the sky rained burning fragments of plastic. Special authorization was also necessary to remove a long line of telephone poles which obstructed the landing pattern of the P-40 Warhawk.

The shot inside the coffeehouse was a set decorator's nightmare.

"I'm taking this in the name of the Fifty-first Pursuit Squadron!" shouted Wild Bill Kelso, and, thus, the rampage began.

Belushi annihilated everything in sight. He broke and emptied every can, jar, and basket. He grabbed and shoved into his gaping mouth anything he could—edible or not! It was an outrageous display of wanton greed and vandalism. For the crew, it was one big belly laugh—Spielberg joked that John might consider starting a fast-food chain specializing in "Belushiburgers"!

John Belushi's stunt double runs from the detonated gas pump.

It was not the only gag centered around food in *1941*. A scene at Malcomb's Cafe, where many main characters were introduced into the story, contained everything from bouncing meatballs to flying turkey legs. And a shot in the Ward's House sequence saw split pea soup splashing across the family dinner table. High cleaning bills eventually convinced many crew members to sport raincoats and galoshes!

Bobby Di Cicco practices his footwork in Malcomb's kitchen (upper left)

Chapter Four

GUESS WHO'S OUT AT SEA?

During the month of December, *1941* was shot concurrently on two Stage 30's, one at Metro-Goldwyn-Mayer and the other at Columbia Pictures Studios. Both involved the same prop, a Japanese submarine. The interior of the vessel was in one location and the full-sized hull was in the other.

Toshiro Mifune and crew interrogate Slim Pickens

"Where Horrywood?"

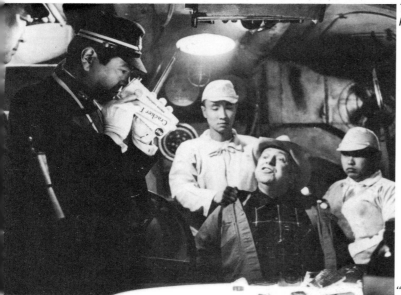

The scenes inside the submarine were not in the original screenplay. Spielberg wanted to increase the screen time of veteran actor Slim Pickens. So he developed a story line that had Pickens playing the unassuming farmer, Hollis Wood, kidnapped and taken hostage by the Japanese. On board the sub were its commander, played by Toshiro Mifune, and a misplaced German officer, portrayed by Christopher Lee.

Spielberg confers with Lee and Mifune

The Japanese crew members used a script specially translated into their native tongue and worked closely with a Japanese translator. A German translator was also always in the wings for Christopher Lee, as their scenes would require English subtitles. Once, when all parties were rehearsing dialogue simultaneously, Spielberg wondered aloud if they were all making the same movie!

The set was a piece of construction best described as rusty and claustrophobic. Spielberg wanted "sweating walls" to enclose the mottled gray navigation chamber, so the crew sweated out six shooting days in the cramped quarters.

To shoot the deck action, the company returned to MGM. Tiny Ocean Pier Park had been dismantled and replaced by a gigantic Japanese submarine replica. Its deck stretched from twenty feet fore of the bow gun to five feet behind the conning tower. It weighed forty tons. Under the hull was a huge, electrically controlled platform that made the sub pitch and rock in ocean motion.

Many scenes were shot in the sub setting: the Japanese crew's reaction to the shelling of the amusement park ("Aiiieee!!"), confrontations between Commander Mitamura and officer Von Kleinschmidt, Wild Bill Kelso's nosedive into the sub's hatch, and a naked young woman's ride on the sub's conning tower periscope.

The periscope on the conning tower of the sub was an independent pneumatic unit. When effects man Logan Frazee opened an air valve, it shot ten feet out of the water before the main portion of the tower rose, a simple procedure compared with surfacing and submerging the sub itself.

For the opening scene of the movie, a difficult maneuver was required. A young female member of the Polar Bear Club (a group of health enthusiasts who prefer swimming the ocean in winter) skinny-dips in the chilly Pacific. Suddenly a gushing fountain of bubbles erupts underneath her and an I-boat periscope rises from the water, carrying her thirty feet into the air!

Actress/stuntwoman Susan Backlinie has a fast and terrifying "rise to the top!"

43

Spielberg wanted the sequence to happen in one master shot. It was to begin with the actress alone in the water and conclude with a full view of the Rising Sun flag emblazoned on the side of the vessel. Toshiro Mifune himself directed most of the crew's astonished reactions to the woman, continually urging them to run about in confusion while remaining militarily formal.

A thirty-six-ton crane was finally engaged to bring the massive structure to the water's surface. The conning tower alone weighed nine thousand pounds. It took numerous false starts and many takes before stuntwoman Susan Backlinie got a chance to dry off. Time and again she was dunked nude into the icy water, wearing no body make-up and requesting only that, with the exception of key personnel, the stage be cleared.

It was the second time Backlinie "went swimming" for Spielberg. Years earlier, in the motion picture *Jaws,* she took a fateful swim into the shark-infested sea. Some people *do* live twice.

A crew is accustomed to being in close proximity to the director and his cameramen, but shooting on the giant submarine mock-up at MGM occurred from up in the rafters, far removed from the activity on the stage floor. Suspended at the end of a long steel arm called a "cherry picker," Spielberg worked from a "basket" that hovered seventy feet over the murky waters. Such a position allowed shots from every conceivable angle—including high shots of the naked Backlinie that would avoid an "R" rating on the picture. In the heavy fog, through which most of the scenes were shot, faces were indistinct and voices muffled.

The company was reunited at a party to celebrate the conclusion of photography. There was sushi and saki for everyone, since the owner of a local Japanese restaurant was so excited at the prospect of meeting Toshiro Mifune that she abandoned her business for the afternoon!

Some of the optical effects employed on *1941* also involved the infamous submarine, and full days were spent shooting just one angle of the sub perched off Ocean Pier Park. Under the supervision of optical effects magicians Bill Abbott, Frank Van der Veer, and Larry Robinson, a system called "front projection" was exercised.

A tremendous piece of the full-sized sub mock-up, the section with the deck gun, rested on movable platforms between a tremendous, highly reflective screen and a crane-mounted projection rig. The Japanese gun crew from MGM and their translator stood on the deck, only this time they were fifteen feet in the air over a dry stage floor.

In the front-projection system, the camera photographs both the live foreground action and a previously filmed scene that is projected onto a screen beyond. Two "tricks" allow the system to work. The first is a Scotchlite front-projection screen, where a normal surface diffuses the light that hits it. Each ray of light that strikes the Scotchlite is reflected in the precise direction from which it came. (This is what made the Scotchlite-covered searchlight beams so bright at Ocean Park.) The second "trick" is a beam-splitting mirror that puts the camera in the perfect position to receive both the image of the live action before it and the reflected image from the screen. When properly aligned, the actors fill their own shadows, and an automatic traveling matte is made in the

Guess Who's Out at Sea?

camera. (A detailed explanation of the process can be found in *The Techniques of Special Effects Cinematography* by Raymond Fielding, Hastings House, 1965.)

The shot in progress was watched through a video reflex camera similar to the one on the Louma. Since the screen reflected the projection part of the image directly back to the camera, the only place the composite scene would be viewed during filming was on the video monitor. The roll of the sub on the platform and smoke (fog) drifting through the stage added to the overall match of what had been shot at MGM. To further tie the background (Ocean Pier Park) to the Japanese gun crew, the deck cannon was made to fire just before a building in the projected park exploded. The result was a structure blown up in October by a shell fired in January of the next year!

Ever since *1941* began, visual effects supervisor Robinson had been working to facilitate its optical effects work. After the success with the front-projection shoot on the sub deck, the next optical project entailed a "movie within a movie."

On Valentine's Day, 1979, the company shot downtown at the Los Angeles Theatre (known as the Hollywood State Theatre in 1941). The purpose was to film the scene of General Stilwell and his entourage enjoying Walt Disney's *Dumbo*. Unbeknownst to all of them is the outbreak of rioting outside in the streets.

Dumbo actually played its premiere engagement on Hollywood Boulevard in December 1941. In his memoirs, Stilwell mentioned seeing it there and forgetting for just a moment about the war. Writers Zemeckis and Gale's inspiration for the scene came from that incident.

Filming a movie while it is being projected is usually not successful. To make the *Dumbo* projection bright and clear, the theater was fitted with a high-gain 2X screen, a projection screen twice as bright as a normal one. The theater projector ran in sync with the *'41* camera so that the image did not flicker. The footage of *Dumbo,* legally obtained from Walt Disney Productions, bounced so brightly off the screen that it almost hurt the eyes!

Normally the theater would be filmed with a blank screen, and the on-screen movie image would be added later by an optical effect of double exposure. The drawback of doing a shot in such a manner is that the camera cannot move. Also, nothing in the foreground may eclipse the screen image without the addition of a hand-animated matte.

1941's 2X screen allowed Bill Fraker's camera to move as much as desired *Dumbo* was seen partially blocked by silhouetted actors and through a haze of cigarette smoke.

When the *1941/Dumbo* footage was viewed the next day, lab personnel familiar with visual effects remarked to Spielberg that the image of the flying elephant was so luminous it looked like an optical. For Robinson, the taste of success was doubly sweet!

Chapter Five

RIOTING ON HOLLYWOOD BOULEVARD

For a brief interlude during the preproduction phase of *1941,* the crew anticipated that Hollywood Boulevard in Hollywood would be a location site for one of the film's major scenes. Investigation of its feasibility took them to the door of Los Angeles Mayor Tom Bradley's office. Meetings were held with city officials, who, for the most part, were enthusiastic about Steven Spielberg's invading downtown. It meant revenue and publicity for Hollywood that money couldn't buy.

Members of *'41's* production company proposed hundreds of necessary period alterations. To name a few, white-line traffic dividers had to be painted out, traffic signals and parking meters had to be changed, and all commercial signs, posters, and billboards had to be replaced by period props.

Despite the possibilities of remarkable production value, the undertaking proved mind-boggling even on paper. Permits, security, crowd control, rerouting traffic, and fully restoring that section of Hollywood to its prewar state would take a year of preparation. *1941* did not have the luxury of time. More prudent plans were constituted for transforming a deserted street on the Columbia Pictures lot into Hollywood Boulevard.

Scheduling problems that left the company with nowhere else to go prompted a mad rush to complete the studio set. After an announcement on a Friday that filming on the location would commence on Monday, crews worked around the clock throughout the weekend. Even when shooting began, construction crews labored out of camera range in every corner.

When it all came to life, it was truly a sight to behold, a trip back in time. Demanding total authenticity, production designer Dean Mitzner had secured actual building plans from the Hollywood Chamber of Commerce. Some were so old they could not be released from the archives for fear they would crumble.

Storefronts were painted in colors exclusive to the '40's, windows displayed furniture and toys that could not be purchased in 1979, and mannequins were dressed in the peak of '40's fashion. Every stop signal, parking meter, billboard, and vehicle parked on the street were historically accurate.

"A set as big and detailed as Hollywood Boulevard could not have been built without the talents of the best in the business," commented production manager John Wilson. "It was a tremendous example of one hundred percent cooperation from the crew and the studio. Everyone was willing to give

Spielberg whatever he wanted—even on the grandest of scales—at a moment's notice."

And a grand scale of events it was. Some of *1941*'s biggest action scenes were shot on the Hollywood Boulevard set, and it took nearly a month to get it all on film.

Every night of photography entailed monumental logistics. Assistant directors Jerry Zeismer and Chris Soldo were often responsible for hundreds of individuals at once: for example, when a big riot scene called for over 650 battling military men, Soldo had to secure the mandatory four pages of employment paperwork on each. Later, producer Buzz Feitshans had to sign his name to each set of papers. Before the movie was over, Feitshans assigned his signature over five thousand times to *1941*-related documents.

THE MAKING OF 1941

Costuming for this set was stunning. Designer Deborah Nadoolman and her crew dressed each actor down to period tie clips and earrings. Zoot-suiters with pink, orange, green, and purple "reat pleats" and "stuffed cuffs" stole the show. Stiff competition came from the military men in period uniforms representing every rank of the United States armed forces.

On the second night of shooting, the massive collection of 650 actors was assembled in a sound stage adjacent to the street set. Sailors, soldiers,

Production illustration of the Hollywood Boulevard sequence

Marines, and zoot-suiters drank gallons of coffee to keep warm and played cards to keep busy while they waited to be summoned into action. A glance at the mob made it obvious that every available extra in Hollywood willing to have his hair shorn was working on the movie. Though they were a congenial group off the set, their on-camera scene was one of violent confrontation, a riot outside the USO dance hall. It was just another result of the hysteria gripping war-nervous America.

Shouting to be heard over the crowd, stunt coordinator Terry Leonard and the assistant directors organized their co-workers, while Spielberg rehearsed the huge group over and over again. Every person involved had to fully understand positioning and reaction to what was happening around him. If he failed to do so, the chances of being cut, bruised, and trampled were doubled.

This riot master shot was an incredibly complex one, an awesome panorama of bodies and crashing automobiles. Film directors George Lucas

and Francis Ford Coppola joined other spectators to witness the scene's execution.

When the action began, most of the extras waited inside the USO building while the streets of Hollywood hosted multiple car collisions. Stuntmen dressed as the Chicano zooters fell from the automobiles like tenpins. Then Spielberg directed a giant fire truck into the intersection, signaling the 650 uniformed men onto the street in a blur of black and blue, punching, kicking, and sprawling bodies. The mob seemed realistically threatening when, cued by Spielberg, executive producer John Milius fired a Thompson rifle to disperse the maddening crowd. As the tremendous herd stampeded from the intersection, ground vibration and the sight of the pandemonium actually caused some spectators to run involuntarily from the set! Visually, the scene had a remarkably powerful psychological effect.

The only other time such a mob scene occurred was at mealtime. Feeding the hundreds of people involved with *1941* was a mammoth job: 79,912 meals were served, and Steven Spielberg himself must have consumed twenty gallons of tea during shooting.

Named Lulubelle after Humphrey Bogart's tank in the movie *Sahara*, *1941*'s M3 Lee tank played a major role in the scene outside the USO. Invisibly commandeered by vehicle expert Pat Carmen, Lulubelle carried Dan Aykroyd and members of his tank crew through the chaos of the riot. Spielberg directed the tank's movements as if conducting an orchestra, and, at one point he accurately positioned the tank before the Hollywood State Theatre, which advertised Walt Disney's *Dumbo*. Inside, General Stilwell, portrayed by Robert Stack, sat oblivious to the havoc outside.

This evening's spectacle was the destruction of the theater's and the adjacent USO's beautiful neon marquees. *Ten thousand feet* of neon had been bent for the two, and they flashed brilliantly in period hues before the camera. Rigging the marquees to break apart when hit by Lulubelle's gunfire was a time-consuming job and Spielberg wanted the action in one take. He got his wish. Under attack, the neon masterpieces exploded in a rush of sparks, smoke, and electrical fireballs, and the entire set became an inferno.

When Spielberg called "Cut!" fire-fighting grips, electricians, and effects men sprang forward with fire extinguishers. But not before Spielberg had shot a living-room version of the scene before him with his super-eight home movie camera.

War had indeed come to Hollywood. The set was nearly obliterated: once resplendent building facades were riddled with bullet holes, the marquees were in pieces, plate-glass windows were smashed and their displays reduced to litter. The rioters had done their worst. Now it was Wild Bill Kelso's turn.

This was to be the last major gag filmed in what once resembled '40's

Sketch of "Uncle Santa's" demise in Hollywood Boulevard sequence

Hollywood. Crazed pilot Wild Bill Kelso (John Belushi) was to crash-land his P-40 Warhawk onto Hollywood Boulevard after being shot down in a dogfight over L.A.

To launch the airplane mock-up, a one-hundred-and-fifty-foot wooden ramp stretched across the Columbia Pictures parking lot, rising fifteen feet above ground and standing safely out of the camera's eye. A. D. Flowers had it rigged so that the craft rode on a small underbelly cart that rolled along the ramp's track. Catapulting the airplane into the air was accomplished by the use of a semi-truck—a towing cable was attached to it and the truck was accelerated to twenty-five miles per hour. With the cables pulley-rigged for a two-to-one ratio, the P-40 would attain a speed of forty mph as it left the ramp.

The effects crew's main headache was that once the plane dislodged, it could not be controlled. It could go anywhere.

The set, closed to visitors, was roped off and security was increased. Too much risk of injury existed. Only twenty stuntpeople were scattered in the path of Wild Bill's maniacal Warhawk. John Belushi's place in the cockpit was taken by a wardrobed mannequin.

At last, the crew breathlessly watched the giant prop fly down the boulevard, hit the street, and glide up to the entrance of the USO. Spielberg's reaction mirrored that of everyone present: the climactic moment was less than sensational. Unfortunately, the towing cable jumped a shiv in the final, crucial pulley and slowed the truck to half its speed. Forced to downshift, transportation coordinator Paul Casella could only get a speed of thirty miles per hour. Consequently, the plane dislodged from the track too slowly. Without the necessary speed, it pancaked to the asphalt.

It hadn't worked. Yet.

A.D. Flowers and his crew

Chapter Six

JITTERBUGGING AT THE USO

"Enthralling" might be the word which best described the interior USO location. Once a nightclub in a residential section of Los Angeles, the site had been converted into *1941*'s home of the Big Band sound and jitterbug mania.

The dazzling decor was inspired by the Deco clubs of old movies and Spielberg's passion for flash. It represented the peak of the creative efforts of both the art and the set decoration departments. Painted in Deco gray, the dance hall had tiered table areas with stainless curved rails rising from the dance floor. The floor itself was a broad expanse of glossy lumber with embossed comic caricatures of Hirohito and Hitler. Overflowing buffet tables graced the wall alongside the bandstand of Sal Stewart's Orchestra and their Serenaders, the Anderson Sisters. A towering Christmas tree adorned the hall, and holiday banners stretched across the ceiling. Everything sparkled with the aid of abounding neon. One wall was nearly covered by an extraordinary American flag fashioned in red, white, and blue fluorescent tubing. This display alone contained one thousand bulbs. Best of all was a huge, hanging mirrored sculpture of a dancing sailor and his partner.

Life on the location was two weeks of concentrated moviemaking in Hollywood's best musical tradition. Despite the close working quarters, excitement for the scene's action kept spirits high and tempers under wraps. This would be the site of the whopping jitterbug dance contest and the onset of the riot.

Penny Marshall as Miss Fitzroy instructs the girls in their jobs as USO hostesses

60

Many of the actors had been in dance rehearsals for twelve weeks prior to the shooting. Choreographer Paul de Rolf worked with them day after day to perfect their movements, focusing on Bobby Di Cicco and Dianne Kay. The talented choreographer brought both from nondancing status to the level of smash jitterbug contest winners.

But the real stars of the show, however, were de Rolf's team of dancers, affectionately called "Buggettes." The eight couples mastered some of the most physically demanding routines ever attempted in a motion picture. Their conventional dancing skills had to be augmented with difficult acrobatics for the dance spectacle. Exhibition splits, flips, and "round-the-back's" had to be perfected. Just watching them was exhausting and even a bit frightening—it was easy to get hurt, and many of the actors sported knee and elbow pads for protection.

The "Buggettes" in a specialty dance number

Treat Williams in mid-brawl

The worst injury was suffered by leading man Treat Williams. During rehearsal of the riot's outbreak, the mirrored ceiling ornament fell from its perch, brushing Williams' face and severely cutting his upper lip. The actor underwent plastic surgery, and for several days of shooting Spielberg had to avoid extreme close-ups of him.

Sickness or injury to a cast member can cause an unexpected and often expensive change in a movie's shooting schedule. Fortunately, with all of *1941*'s extraordinary action sequences, very few injuries were tallied up.

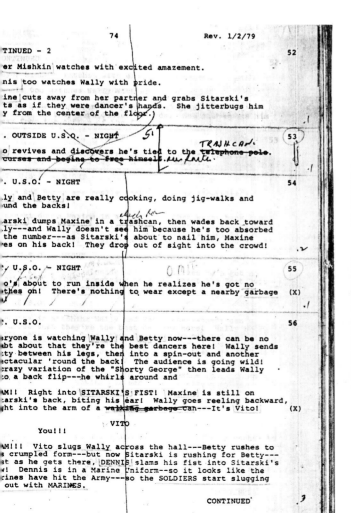

74   Rev. 1/2/79

TINUED - 2   52

er Mishkin watches with excited amazement.

nis too watches Wally with pride.

ine cuts away from her partner and grabs Sitarski's
ts as if they were dancer's hands. She jitterbugs him
y from the center of the floor.)

. OUTSIDE U.S.O. - NIGHT   53

             TRASHCAN.
o revives and discovers he's tied to the ~~telephone pole~~.
~~curses and begins to free himself~~.

. U.S.O. - NIGHT   54

ly and Betty are really cooking, doing jig-walks and
und the backs!

arski dumps Maxine in a trashcan, then wades back toward
ly---and Wally doesn't see him because he's too absorbed
the number---as Sitarski's about to nail him, Maxine
es on his back! They drop out of sight into the crowd!

. U.S.O. - NIGHT   OMIT   55

o's about to run inside when he realizes he's got no
thes on! There's nothing to wear except a nearby garbage (X)

. U.S.O.   56

ryone is watching Wally and Betty now---there can be no
bt about that they're the best dancers here! Wally sends
ty between his legs, then into a spin-out and another
ectacular 'round the back! The audience is going wild!
razy variation of the "Shorty George" then leads Wally
o a back flip---he whirls around and

AMI! Right into SITARSKI'S FIST! Maxine is still on
arski's back, biting his ear! Wally goes reeling backward,
ht into the arm of a ~~walking garbage can~~---It's Vito! (X)

            VITO
   You!!!

AM!! Vito slugs Wally across the hall---Betty rushes to
s crumpled form---but now Sitarski is rushing for Betty---
st as he gets there, DENNIS slams his fist into Sitarski's
w! Dennis is in a Marine Uniform--so it looks like the
rines have hit the Army---so the SOLDIERS start slugging
  out with MARINES.

           CONTINUED

Script supervisor Marie Kenney's shot notations for the Jitterbug contest sequence

Joe Flaherty and Ignatius Wolfington

Finally the camera setup was complete, and the assistant directors positioned all of the scene's performers. Time for jitterbug fever.

Suave bandleader Sal Stewart, played by Joe Flaherty, conducted the festivities clutching the microphone in a two-fisted embrace. Sharing center stage was RKO talent scout Meyer Mishkin, played by Ignatius Wolfington, as well as the "Anderson Sisters," a trio of actress-singers who exuded 40's style and rosy-cheeked verve.

The "Anderson Sisters": Marjorie Gaines, Trish Garland, and Carol Culver

Jitterbugging at the USO

Over one hundred and fifty period-coiffed and -wardrobed patrons jammed the dance floor and packed the galleries. Cameras rolled and *1941*'s dancers became a phenomenon of motion. The main ensemble dance, a tendon-wrenching routine, was repeated for hours at a time. Di Cicco and Kay maneuvered through the formation like seasoned professionals, both stretching into seemingly effortless leaps and scissorlike splits. When they exited center stage, the Buggettes emerged in an acrobatic display of synchronized motion, their complex gyrations achieving the "Jitterbug Nirvana" noted in the script. Director Spielberg and Cameraman Fraker were visibly pleased.

One disappointment was the need to abandon an overhead camera angle. Spielberg had hoped to shoot straight down, in Busby Berkeley-style, at the configuration of dancers. Unfortunately, even with the Louma, the camera could not crane high enough because of ceiling-height restrictions. Another limitation was the inability to get a satisfactory Panavision composition.

"You can do anything in the Academy ratio (television) and almost anything in the standard 1:85 ratio (modern movies), but in Panavision, getting a decent composition is a constant struggle," acknowledged Spielberg. The envisioned "June Taylor Snowflake" consequently melted into oblivion.

When the sequence progressed to the scripted Di Cicco-Williams pursuit scene, more elements of risk were added to the already considerable strain. At one point, the dancers did ankle-twisting stunt moves for the hundredth time while Di Cicco, Williams, Dianne Kay, and Wendie Jo Sperber threaded in and out of the action. They came dangerously close to the whirling heels of the Buggettes. Di Cicco caught a flying young dancer who straddled him at the

waist. He tossed her to Williams, who was knocked flat by the impact. When Williams stood up, he was caught between the legs of another dancer, who was being spun dervish-style. The trick worked, but courageous Treat Williams had to nurse a still tender lip. All the men and women in the USO sequence were as resilient as tempered steel, human medicine balls at one time or another, and the pace eased for no one.

Spielberg, Fraker, choreographer de Rolf, and the effects crew continually staged the scene's action. One tricky piece of filming incorporated a 360-degree circular track around the dance formation. The camera swung in a full arc while the dancers peeled like an orange to reveal contest winners Di Cicco and Kay in center stage. The camera operators, grips, and electricians really had their talents taxed in two pieces of action prior to the riot scene, while, from Louma control, Spielberg choreographed a dozen variables that concluded in perhaps the most ingenious gag in the scene.

Bobby Di Cicco was to leap from the bandstand to the buffet table in flight from Treat Williams. Then, with moves to rival Fred Astaire, Di Cicco was to tap-dance down the table's twenty-foot length, never crushing a single pastry or disturbing a piece of silverware. The wrinkle was that Bobby could not tap-dance, but after weeks of careful planning and special effects rigging, the audience would be successfully fooled.

A. D. Flowers affixed a rolling trapeze to the hall ceiling above the refreshment table. Di Cicco would leap to the table and hoist himself onto the trapeze that hung invisible to the camera. Choreographer de Rolf, a professional tapper, would drop to the table from his hidden perch on the trapeze. For a successful switch of feet, the timing had to be exact. Twenty-one (!) takes later, the gag was on the mark.

The Rube Goldberg-style gag

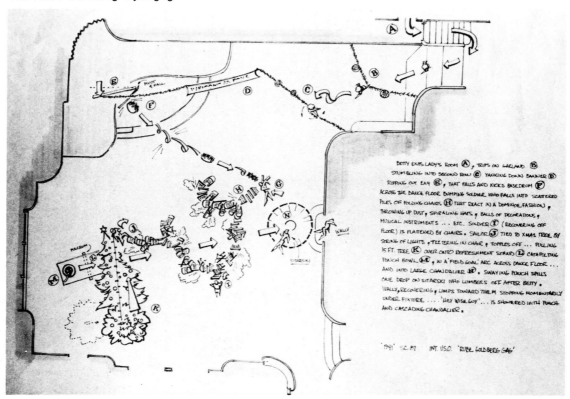

One more Excedrin headache for the effects crew was to bring to life one of illustrator Jensen's most detailed sketches. Written into the USO's outbreak of havoc was a Rube Goldberg-style gag. A. D. Flowers rigged an incredibly intricate series of events. First, panic-stricken Dianne Kay emerged from the ladies' room to witness the riot's destruction. The heel of her shoe caught on a piece of Christmas garland. The garland pulled down the USO banner strung across the top of the stage. A two-by-four attached to the banner smashed through the bandstand. The bass drum rolled off the stage, down the stairs, and across the dance floor, striking a stack of folding chairs that fell to the floor in a domino reaction. The last toppled chair contained an unconscious sailor who had a string of Christmas lights wrapped around him. Since the lights were still attached to the fifteen-foot Christmas tree, the sailor fell off the seat and toppled the tree. The tree hit the damaged refreshment table and catapulted a bowl of punch through the air until it landed in a crystal chandelier. The side-heavy light fixture tilted, splashing only a single drop of punch on the unconscious face of Treat Williams, who was sprawled on the floor. Flowers and his men dared anyone to quip, "All in a day's work."

Director Spielberg stages the outbreak of the riot

The outbreak of the riot took a few days to film. This scene was filled with more concentrated "cartoon violence" than any other one in the movie. As the script declared: "The Great Zoot-Suit Riot of 1941 was on!"

The very first punch was thrown by actor James Caan, who happened by the set on that fateful day. Persuaded by Spielberg to join in the fun, he was rushed into appropriate Navy attire. Stunt coordinator Leonard and his crew responded to sailor Caan by methodically demolishing everything in sight. Two hundred period-designed chairs were reduced to wood chips, musical instruments were bent beyond recognition, every piece of decor was ripped from its glue, windows were smashed into bits of sand, and doors were broken

James Caan

71

into matchsticks. Hidden trampolines somersaulted stuntmen in wild arcs over the heads of the brawling combatants. The slugfest then moved to the street, at which point the action stopped. The next scene, in which the entire armed forces enlarged the melee, had already been shot.

At last the soldiers stripped off their constricting uniforms and the USO hostesses unpinned fancy curls and washed off pancake make-up. The jitterbuggers massaged tired ankles and hummed Beethoven. It was finally over.

Treat Williams and Wendie Jo Sperber,
when the battle's over

Jitterbugging at the USO

Chapter Seven

CROWDED SKIES

In the brisk month of February the production company convened on a concrete apron adjacent to the Long Beach Airport to film the antihysteria speech to the press by General Stilwell, played by Robert Stack.

A small air force had been rented for background. When Stack marched solemnly across the tarmac, the Louma-mounted camera weaved with him through the impressive collection of war planes. Six T6 trainers were rented from a local sky-writing team. Also present were three B-25 Mitchell bombers. One had been the executive plane of General Dwight Eisenhower. But the most

eye-catching piece was the huge silver bird parked at the far end of the field. A stupendous B-17 bomber, loaned by the Confederate Air Force, served as the rendezvous spot for Captain Birkhead (Tim Matheson) and General Stilwell's secretary, Donna Stratton (Nancy Allen).

The Long Beach Airport runways added to the production value of the shot, though airplane noise levels did occasionally interfere with sound mixer Gene Cantamessa's efforts to record an audible sound track.

Nancy Allen and Tim Matheson rendezvous under a B-17 bomber

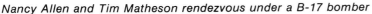

The general's car explodes

The scene's biggest day of shooting was both anxious and numbing. A huge explosion effect was required as the result of a runaway bomb. In the script, Matheson and Allen, alone at last in the B-17, tangled in an impassioned embrace. A bomb-bay door switch was accidentally bumped, and out dropped its contents. The defense bomb rolled across the airfield and pitched toward General Stilwell and the assembled press. Its path cleared, the bomb triggered

a fiery blast upon impact with the grandstands. Spielberg wanted the scene to surpass the earlier shot of the detonation of Wild Bill's refueling station.

Aside from rigging the wooden benches to blow, the effects men created an ear-ringing blast of kerosene and mortars to flip Stilwell's car and the surrounding military vehicles. As sometimes happens with big, complicated effects rigs, the simplest of their ingredients can fail to perform. When the tremendous explosion occurred, the general's car remained parked. After picking apart the rubble piece by piece, the crew found that the automobile's battery was dead. An additional day in the production schedule was required to repeat the blast.

This was not the only major sight gag done a second time. After viewing the film of Wild Bill Kelso's crash into Hollywood Boulevard, Spielberg was not satisfied, and decided to shoot the estimated half-million-dollar gag again.

In the forty-five days since the initial crash, the P-40 Warhawk had been craftily restored to its prefall state. The elevated launching track sported nearly a hundred additional feet of rail. With the Hollywood Boulevard set still in its devastated condition, all that required attention was the aircraft's path. Effects men scattered burning paraffin chips everywhere to dress the street in firebrands resulting from the riot. On the opposite side of the set, driver Casella again test-drove two semi-trucks to determine which would tow the airplane-attached cable.

Each individual camera operator was instructed to yell only if his camera did *not* roll. Security was exceptionally heavy, and the privileged spectators were herded a good distance from the crash site. A pool was formed to bet just where the impact point would be.

Then, a great whirring noise was heard from the darkness beyond. The P-40 hurtled down the roller-coaster track at forty-five miles per hour and separated cleanly at the fuselage. When it hit the street and slid up to the USO's entrance, its momentum was that of a locomotive. This time there was no doubt—the impact was stupendous.

"What's this?" Spielberg questioned when a bundle of bills was shoved into his palm. Spielberg himself had won the plane-crash pool. The P-40 hit right where the director said it would.

The magic of Hollywood allowed *1941*'s in-flight scenes to be photographed right on the ground.

A gimbal is a large steel assembly approximately twelve feet square and eight feet tall. It consists of a wide base supporting two sets of hooplike rockers. When activated, these rockers force whatever sits atop the base to be moved in every direction.

On a stage at the Burbank studios, the P-40 Warhawk was mounted on this contraption. One lever tipped the aircraft's nose up and down, another tilted the wings left and right. When both levers were manipulated simultaneously, the plane had the appearance of being realistically airborne. Smoke pots and ritter fans pumped to give the illusion of clouds.

With the Louma camera arm swung upward and over the P-40's wing, Spielberg was able to get close-up shots of cigar-chomping Wild Bill Kelso at the controls.

It was good to have John Belushi back on the set. Having spent months crisscrossing the country twice a week to accommodate both *1941* and *Saturday Night Live*'s shooting schedules, he was at home in an airplane.

Robert Stack, John Belushi and Nancy Allen in a relaxed moment on the set

The wing-mounted machine guns were actually powered from the stage floor. When Belushi's guns fired, a spinning valve in each device alternated between omitting a propane blast from the barrel and igniting it with a spark plug. The result was a rapid-fire rat-tat-tat of muzzle flames that resembled real wing guns in operation. Spielberg originally requested real guns that would shoot tracer bullets, but A. D. Flowers assured him the United States government would shoot the idea right down.

1941's midair romantic interlude was also shot on the stage. But the Beechcraft trainer was more difficult to balance on the gimbal than the smaller P-40. In its rocking interior, Nancy Allen and Tim Matheson grappled hungrily, unaware they were being taken for enemy aircraft. The fun was momentarily delayed while the plane's careful prerigging was activated. Bundles of foot-wide wires were crammed into the rear of the passenger compartment and connected to individual bullet hits. Rows of holes had been punched into the aluminum skin, charges placed, and the holes refilled. Inside were pre-aimed mortars that shot small ballbearings cleanly through the windscreen. On cue, the plane began to disintegrate around the embracing duo. According to the script, Allen and Matheson were virtually under attack by Belushi!

Sound stages were a common location for the shooting of uncommon sequences. Actors David Lander and Michael McKean, alias Lenny and Squiggy of television's *Laverne and Shirley,* participated in such a piece of drama, portraying Willy and Joe, two soldiers named after the famous cartoon

characters of Bill Mauldin. Later, a second team of flak gunners was called Hanley and Saunders, whose names were taken from the television series *Combat!*

Clothed in Army fatigues and doughboy helmets, Lander and McKean sat perched atop an antiaircraft gun in the middle of a Hollywood Boulevard rooftop. The set, constructed on another stage at Columbia Pictures, had to tie in with the actual street set. To accomplish the task, visual effects supervisors Abbott, Van der Veer, and Robinson erected a tremendous blue screen on one side of the stage. Later, when the Hollywood Boulevard miniature was shot, a tiny vista would be matted into the blue area—thus placing Lander and McKean three floors up over the street!

Crowded Skies

Van der Veer had done hundreds of such opticals so efficiently that, with a bit of extra care, he could produce traveling matte shots of extremely high quality, devoid of the telltale blue lines that stand out in so many motion pictures.

To demonstrate to Spielberg how well the blue-screen matte could work, a composite test was made using a shot from Ocean Pier Park as background material. The two gunners looked rather absurd on a rooftop half a mile out in the ocean, but the shot sold the director on the process. Quite a job just to show two homesick GI's dreaming of shooting the moon out of the sky rather than being war heroes!

THE MAKING OF 1941

Chapter Eight

AIR RAID ON L.A.

Back in the early '40's, when invasion was considered a serious threat, Interceptor Command was the hub of Los Angeles' civil defense network. It was a communications center connected by telephone to the hundreds of air raid wardens and civil defense spotters stationed throughout Southern California. All aircraft sightings were called into this intelligence clearinghouse, plotted on a table map, and checked against *listed* flight plans. If an air raid was in progress, hoards of antiaircraft batteries in the general Los Angeles area would receive instructions from this command center.

    1941's post was in a basement-style building that had the look of a bomb shelter. Banks of telephones manned by rows of sober aides dressed the authentic set. A giant map for plotting aircraft movement over California was strategically placed in full view of all employees. Lights of different colors denoted the level of alert.

Interceptor Command Headquarters

Sam Fuller (l.) and staff at Interceptor Command

Spielberg conferred with writer-director-producer Sam Fuller, who was persuaded to play the commanding officer of Interceptor Command, and was transformed into the subdued, jaw-locked leader. He exhaled terse war commands similar to those he himself had written and directed for years.

The scene itself was short and direct. The Beechcraft joy ride of Matheson and Allen suddenly registered as unidentifiable activity. Leaning over the broad plotting map, Sam Fuller belted out: "Go to Red Alert! Red Alert for Los Angeles! RED ALERT!"

Thus, the Great Los Angeles Air Raid began.

Scenes of interior tank action were shot at the nearby CBS Studios, where an interior tank mock-up just large enough to hold the crew and some unexpected guests was erected on a stage. The effects crew simulated a rough ride for Lulubelle by rocking the steel-framed hotbox with off-camera levers. Jostled and shaken, the cast labored in vain to untangle themselves from one another. Spielberg frequently rearranged them to do plenty of painstaking crawling and struggling for even an extra inch.

Shooting the tank interiors

Cramped inside the tank

Caught once again in the middle of it all was Dianne Kay, whose biggest feat was making herself heard over the clucking of five loudmouthed hens that found their way into the tank.

Dan Aykroyd was fairly quiet at this point. Most of the scene found him knocked unconscious from the Hollywood Boulevard riot encounter. He was jarred awake when some chicken byproducts dropped into his commander's seat.

"Chicken SHIT!" rang through the rafters. Aykroyd echoed the cast and crew's similar sentiments about barnyard working conditions.

Spielberg sympathized. "Lose the chickens. It's getting too FOWL in here!"

The nights at CBS were spent outside shooting the exteriors of Lulubelle en route from Hollywood to Ocean Park. In hot pursuit was a motorcycle and sidecar with stunt doubles for its passengering lead actors. The highlight of the location was the effects department's destruction of a police prowl car. Eager to find a target for their machine gun, Lulubelle's entourage paused to shoot the automobile to pieces because its headlights were on during the declared blackout! When the tank's gun started to shoot, the car's windows were riddled. While squib charges punched holes in the doors and bodywork, power-fired rams kicked the entire car apart in precut sections. The fenders, the doors, the roof, were all knocked free until the vehicle finally caved in. Only the two headlights, the intended targets, were left untouched and glowing in the darkness!

Air Raid on L.A.

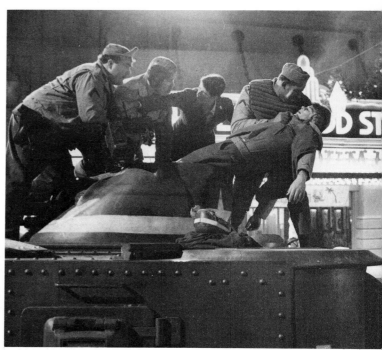

THE MAKING OF 1941

Air Raid on L.A.

Eddie Deezen

Suddenly Spielberg decided the tank needed a colorful side trip on its voyage to the sea, to an abandoned paint factory, and another sequence was born and added to *1941*'s already elongated schedule.

"Heyyy … where is everybody?" The stage was so full of smoke from the Navy fogger that Eddie Deezen had to yell to find his way across the set. He and Murray Hamilton portrayed the *real* air raid wardens, Herb and Claude. Their miniature stand-ins had already been dipped into the waves on the stage at MGM. Eddie and Murray's scenes atop the full-sized Ferris wheel would be cut into the spectacular miniatures of Ocean Park and its giant wheel.

Shooting script describing the Ferris wheel's destruction

Spielberg directs Murray Hamilton, Eddie Deezen and the dummy

On a Columbia sound stage stood one half of the amusement-park ride. The highest seat was only twelve feet above the floor for accessible filming. Dressed up in overcoats, winter hats, and rain boots, the pair acted out a classic slapstick-comedy routine while swinging to and fro in the Ferris-wheel seat. Hamilton played the suffering straight man of the team—cold, miserable, afraid of heights, and nauseated by his partner!

Murray Hamilton and Eddie Deezen (Little Deez is between them).

Deezen's comic persona was a gangly, awkward, distraught wacko. Queasy from the height, Hamilton watched helplessly as the enthusiastic Deezen rocked the seat and chattered incessantly about vertigo and the good odds of an accident.

Sharing the scenes with the two was a ventriloquist's dummy, a clever extension of Eddie's character. The dummy (nicknamed "Little Deez") looked exactly like the actor. At first ignoring the wisecracking dummy, Hamilton finally began to actually listen to him, accepting him as a separate person. According to the script, Little Deez was the first one to spot the Japanese sub, and when Hamilton saw it, too, he shouted: "Holy shit, Herb, the dummy's right!"

Within a week a hefty supply of Spielberg-ordered T-shirts arrived for the crew, embossed with that phrase of dialogue!

These T-shirts weren't the first, either. For fun, for publicity, and for whatever reason someone could dream up, nearly fifteen thousand (!) T-shirts were made for the movie.

The man behind the dummy was ventriloquist Jerry Layne. He operated the sculpture in all shots with the exception of those showing the space directly beneath the Ferris-wheel seat. Standing on a ladder, he manipulated the eyes, ears, nose, and mouth of the figure through a hole in the seat.

Spielberg and Jerry Layne, who operated the dummy

The half-wheel was later exchanged for an operational whole wheel, signaling the scenes showing Hamilton, Deezen, and the dummy hanging on while the burning Ferris wheel rolled off its gantry. The effects department lit smoke pots in the wheel's seats and exploded shell hits as the wheel turned.

Everyone hits the water: the tank crew, the air-raid wardens, even Wild Bill Kelso

To make the wheel appear to be rolling out of control, the Louma was mounted so that it could be rocked from side to side as it pointed at the turning wheel. On the Louma control monitor it looked as though the wheel and not the camera was doing the rocking. The terrified faces of the two actors flew by the camera.

The latest on-the-set talk concerned guesses at when *1941* would *end.* The extra months of unexpected shooting had added up. The crew was anxious and made their feelings known by producing yet another T-shirt. Definitely the most popular and perhaps the most appropriate, it read: "1941 Forever . . . and ever . . . and ever."

On the back lot of Columbia Pictures was the acreage used by television's *The Waltons.* Its geography included a large, egg-shaped pond rimmed by ample trees and brush which, for *1941,* became Los Angeles' famous La Brea Tar Pits.

Director's sketch of the La Brea Tar Pits

SC-221 (E)
MASTER LA BREA TAR PIT SHOT - COMPOSITE MATTE

TAR POOL #2

The water was drained from the water hole and filled with Bentinite. Gooey and jet-black in color, this substance is used for purposes ranging from a lubrication for oil rigs to a base for cosmetics. The special effects department rigged air and steam pipes under the Bentinite to produce a bubbling, hissing effect. It sounded like a devil's cauldron, and colored lights in hues of green, red, and orange contributed to the "Lost World" feeling of the set.

To fully resemble the prehistoric tar pools, *1941*'s two biggest decorative props were positioned in the mire. Measuring over forty feet long and twenty-five feet high stood a dinosaur and a tyrannosaurus rex. Both were award-

winning pieces of sculpture. Designed by Pillsbury Doughboy creator Eric Von Buelow, their gaping jaws sufficiently terrorized crash-landing survivors Nancy Allen and Tim Matheson—who were also a sight to behold. As a result of the accident, Spielberg instructed that they both be tarred and feathered almost beyond recognition. Their costumes were a mass of dripping black gook, and Allen's golden curls stuck to her cheeks. The actress seemed a bit self-conscious about her disheveled appearance off-camera, but Matheson incorporated the unusual look into his characteristic clowning around.

When Bill Fraker was ready, the two actors entered the submerged Beechcraft by walking a plank extended across the pit. The set, dressed for the immediacy of the crash, looked like Dante's *Inferno.* A speaker mounted near the Louma lens allowed Spielberg to direct his actors from Louma control rather than from within the tar itself.

Shortly before the final take, controlled flames licking the far side of the fuselage ignited something inside the Beechcraft. Allen and Matheson were unable to breathe inside the smoky interior until the plank was replaced and help arrived. It was a small fire and a big scare for all present.

Air Raid on L.A.

Chapter Nine

A VISIT TO WARD'S HOUSE

Steven Spielberg repeatedly called the Ward's House sequence of *1941* the most exciting. It was also the largest and most constant challenge of the picture.

Just to secure the location took nearly one year's time. The difficulty centered on the extensive action occurring at the oceanside house itself as well as out at sea. In the script, the home of Ward Douglas was chosen by the United States Army as strategically advantageous for the installation of an aircraft defense battery. They positioned a 40mm antiaircraft gun in Ward's front yard. Mistaken for an industrial structure by a Japanese submarine lurking out at sea, the house is shelled and cartwheeled to the sand and rocks below.

To accommodate the scene, a clifftop house had to be found that would pass as a believable location for borrowing by the armed forces. Also, the surrounding area could not be heavily populated, and the architecture of the neighboring structures had to be of the '40's period.

Sketch of Ward's house

Spielberg studies house model with Art Director Bill O'Brien and Designer Dean Mitzner

It finally became "the house that '41 built."

After months of scouting the western coastline from San Diego to Oregon, an ideal spot was found: a vacant lot perched high above the sands of Southern California. Nothing man-made obstructed the setting. It was perfect— and the California Coastal Commission thought so, too.

Just north of Malibu, California, lay the stretch of surf called Nicholas Beach. After extensive negotiations with the Coastal Commission and with numerous other state agencies, *1941* won the right to use it as a practical shooting location.

The land had been appropriated for a new state beach seasons earlier. The authorities were very sensitive to preserving the beauty of the locale. The movie company was neither to disturb the land nor to impair public use of the beach. The Coastal Commission issued strong warnings that *1941* could not so much as crush a sliver of ice plant or rearrange a piece of driftwood.

What the set had in beauty it lacked in space. Transportation organized the company vehicles as best it could on the one narrow road that threaded

through the set. The trucks needed to be close by but also had to be easily hidden when the cameras faced inland. The "neighbor's" house on the hill above the set was actually a false front and served double duty to camouflage the wardrobe and make-up trailers. The *only* telephone was up there as well.

Although some of the familiar cast members from the Hollywood Boulevard scenes could be seen relaxing in the sunshine, the number of new faces at the beach house gave the impression that the company was embarking on a whole new movie. As Ward Douglas, patriotic taxpayer and all-around family man, Ned Beatty was a vibrant presence. Lorraine Gary, playing Ward's wife, Joan, matched Beatty in charm and candor. She had worked with Spielberg before on *Jaws,* and once again he cast her in the role of a housewife living by the sea. Against overwhelming forces, the energetic woman would battle in slapstick effort to save her home.

The Douglas family was the "white bread" of *1941.* Respectably patriotic, wholesome, and content, it was the perfect target for Invasion Hysteria.

Lionel Stander, a character actor whose career dated back to the '30's comedy, filled the role of the Douglases' Italian-American neighbor, Mr. Scioli. Stander told the best stories on the set. Retained in his sharp memory were five decades of Hollywood history. Stander was also one of the few people on the set who could drive a 1941 car!

Dianne Kay played daughter Betty, and three rascal boys rounded out the Douglas clan. Jordan Brian, Steven Mond, and Christian Zika acted as the

Lionel Stander

freckle-faced brothers. The eldest wore the uniform of the Boy Rangers—while finalizing some characters and costumes earlier in the production, Spielberg had been denied usage of the name, uniform, and insignia of the Boy Scouts of America (to which the organization holds all rights). Stumped for a youth organization, Spielberg remembered the Boy Rangers. Any movie buff worth his or her popcorn would recognize the group as the boys' club in Frank Capra's *Mr. Smith Goes to Washington.* As with Lulubelle and *Sahara,* the film classic was a Columbia production. *1941* could use the Boy Rangers without any repercussions.

By reshuffling script pages, Spielberg often made major changes in *1941* during filming. Scenes were dropped and new ones added. In exchange for an omission, a scene was added to the already complex Ward's House sequence.

Bobby Di Cicco, as love-crazed Wally, hid in the rafters of the Douglases' garage amid garden tools and fertilizer.

Spielberg staged the first scene shot on the location in an involved master shot. Twenty-two takes later, it was a print, the highest-take shot of the movie. Spielberg had continued to reshoot the scene until he was completely satisfied with the way his frequent corrections had helped the scene develop in the direction he wanted it to go.

Ward's house gave the crew another opportunity to watch Dan Aykroyd. As

"The Magnificent Five"

Sergeant Tree, he and his motor-pool crew delivered the antiaircraft gun to the Douglases' front yard. The soldiers were a sorry sight, a formation of sad sacks. Treat Williams satirically dubbed his comrades "the Magnificent Five"!

While the five crazy guys climbed on the gun like a jungle gym, Aykroyd gave Beatty an inadvertent artillery lesson. He told him what *not* to touch on the big green 40mm piece. Then, a baton was passed to Aykroyd, who stepped onto the carriage and delivered a point-by-point demo speech in the style he used for his bogus *Saturday Night Live* commercials.

"Whatever you do, do not depress this lever here, and upon no account should you follow that action by pushing this black release button, thusly . . ." Perfectly clear, of course.

Beatty paid careful attention. To family leader Ward, the gun was more than a weapon: it was a symbol. It provided him with the opportunity to overcome his feeling of helplessness, of having no place in the Second World War. It made him a hero.

Across the laundry line from the action, Betty (Dianne Kay) and best friend Maxine (Wendie Jo Sperber) had fallen into a hole the boys had dug in the center of the front yard. The little ankle-biters (Aykroyd's line) called the pit a "Jap trap," the younger generation's chosen method of defense!

Williams sauntered to the rescue of the ladies. While he expressed his wolfish affection for Kay, she demanded he keep hands off and put her down. A stuntwoman took her place, and Williams straight-pressed her up into the air and threw her to the bottom of the pit. Effects men had rigged it with stacks of cushions and blew a puff of fuller's earth up after each fall. There was more than one—Spielberg shot the plummet to earth four times before he was completely satisfied.

The child actors on '41 usually played war, even when not working. The three boys would run around the yard toting plastic rifles and shooting slingshots at imaginary soldiers. Eventually they began fighting with one another.

Spielberg inspects the "Jap trap" while Wendie Jo Sperber and Dianne Kay huddle in the bottom

"Where's the kid wrangler?" Spielberg would holler above their heads. He wasn't about to get caught in the middle.

To comply with state labor laws, the company had a studio teacher on the set to conduct studies for the children in between calls. When things got a little rough, assistant director Ziesmer would suddenly announce that school was in session!

At mealtime the company retired to the ocean-view dinner tent. Somehow the tiresome catered food tasted a bit better when consumed surfside. Many crew members would use the break to collapse on the sand for some presummer suntan or to search the horizon with binoculars for whales. After the long weeks of cold night shooting, it was like a vacation: a very short one.

After a few days of sunshine paradise the shooting at the Nicholas Beach house changed over to nights. The purpose was to film Ward Douglas's unsuccessful defense of his home against the enemy. As far back as the Indian Dunes shoot, Spielberg had said that he was intrigued by the idea of a man destroying his own home while trying to defend it. Buster Keaton and Laurel and Hardy no doubt would have agreed.

A. D.'s entire group of effects men had their cables, shock cords, air mortars, and explosives ready to make all the mechanical gags work. Because the interior scenes were later shot in a different location, virtually all of the complicated effects were staged twice.

Beatty spotted the lurking Japanese submarine from his surfside balcony and was inspired with the idea of sinking it. The 40mm gun, parked in his front yard, would come in handy. But he had only memorized how to fire the gun. He knew neither how to aim it nor how to anchor it properly in place. From then on, almost every shot involved effects work.

The heavy artillery piece was rigged on towing cables to roll. Beatty worked in close-ups while his stunt double rode the rolling gun for the more dangerous shots. Entire walls of the house and garage, built entirely with balsa wood, disintegrated when the gun careened through them. Careful preparations by the art and construction departments paid off as new replacement walls appeared instantly. After a few minutes of attention by carpenters and painters, the set was ready for additional takes.

THE MAKING OF 1941

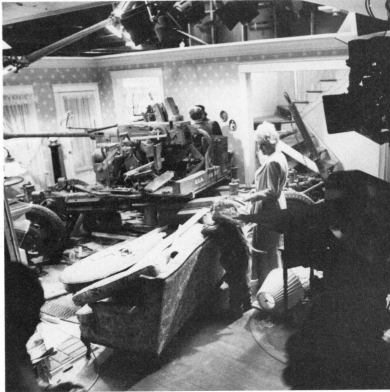

As neighbor Scioli, Stander skeptically complied with Beatty's scatterbrained insistence on getting himself into trouble. Mrs. Scioli, played by Ann Molinari, watched in horror with the rest of the "neighborhood" as her husband helped reset the runaway cannon.

Beatty was not the only one to have gone a little defense-crazy. In his own enthusiasm to get in on the war effort, Scioli had converted his family car into a homemade tank! Covered with sheet metal and barbed wire, it even had a bathtub sitting in its trunk, complete with shower head! The manic mobile had been designed by the effects crew and built at the hangar nearly a year before.

Beatty eventually turned his house into a battlefield. He did not know how to anchor the gun with the round "feet" that in normal use screw down and lift the chassis off the ground! The *1941* company had some problems of its own with the brakes on the gun's wheels. The heavy cannon seemed to get away from the shooting crew as often as it ran loose in the script. At one time the brakes seized up with Beatty himself in the saddle. He cut his forehead when the gun jolted to a halt.

Scioli's homemade "tank"

In a different take with a camera attached to its barrel, the 40mm gun rocketed toward the house. For that particular shot, the carriage was marked to stop at the front door. Unexpectedly, it did not, and with the momentum of a bullet, it smashed through the threshold and piled up on the Douglases' staircase.

Stuntwoman Jeanie Epper, doubling Lorraine Gary, had been standing directly behind the door in every previous take. She miraculously followed an impulse to step clear of the threshold for that specific take. She was lucky to be alive. It was the only instance where an error put a human being in real danger.

The only accidental injury at the location was the result of an incident

A Visit to Ward's House

more ironic than anything else. Associate producer Janet Healy was standing in for a stunt where the gun was fired from inside the house and blew out all the windows. An air mortar at each window popped the breakaway glass out of the frames, and the stuntpeople outside pretended to be knocked down by a shock wave. Healy stood alongside stunt coordinator Terry Leonard. In action, both fell to the ground and Leonard accidentally landed on Healy. Her wrist was in a cast for the remainder of *1941*.

In April the company moved to the Columbia lot, where the interior of the Douglas house had been duplicated on a sound stage. The break gave Logan Frazee and his effects crew time to rig the entire beach house to fall off the cliff. This was to be the climactic effects gag of the movie, the last of the major miracles A. D. Flowers and his men pulled off for *1941*. It was definitely a ridiculous way to take a $260,000 (cost to build) home off the market! And it could be done only once.

The dropping of the house was Frazee's baby. When the company left the beach, it was not prepared in any way for the fall. Frazee had fifteen working days to rig a fail-safe mechanism both to drop the house and to blow it up for the one critical take.

Flowers, meanwhile, was busy redoing most of the effects gags in the house set at Columbia. Breakaway doors, staircases, and interior walls were readied for more destruction as Spielberg filmed the family scenes in the Douglas dining and living rooms.

The dinner scene was a humorous family gathering. Lorraine Gary could

tolerate the dog that took a seat at the table, but not the sight of son Jordan Brian wearing an old-fashioned gas mask to dinner. This was an example of how a simple "touch" could mean a complicated effects job.

Brian dipped the hose part of the mask into his bowl of green pea soup. As the bowl drained, the goggle lenses in the rigged mask were seen to fill slowly with the green liquid. When he pretended to suck, the soup was drained out a little hole at the bottom of the bowl. But the liquid looked as if it were going up into the mask. At the proper moment the effects operator turned a valve that forced more soup up through hidden tubes and into two specially constructed mask lenses. Each lens was actually two glass discs with a space in between. The green pea soup flowed into the space and slowly filled it up. The young actor seemed to be drowning in the stuff, but he was actually as dry as a bone. It was all convincingly repulsive.

For another rather unique mechanical gag, the entire upstairs floor of a bedroom cavalcaded into the middle of the living room. Effects men fired cable cutters that held the free-hanging floor section at ceiling level. With a rush of air and a resounding crash, everything fell spectacularly to the carpet.

Spielberg had used the Louma in the house wherever he could. He hovered over the Louma control video monitor for a take of the cable-rigged 40mm gun crashing through the Douglas front door and splintering the balsa staircase. Beatty's stunt double remained seated on the gun and came through the balsa fragments and cracked plaster with nary a scratch. It was the fourth attempt at the shot, and Spielberg the perfectionist bought it.

For one solid week Spielberg shot and reshot the inside destruction of the house. The special effects department lost count of how many explosions occurred in just the one sequence.

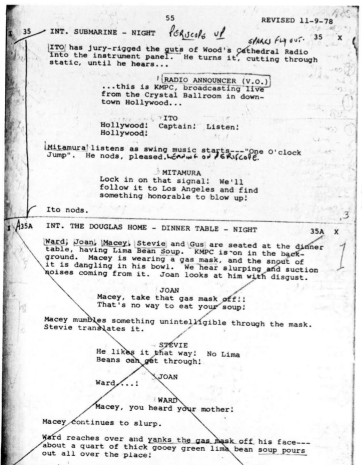

Shooting script notations on the pea soup in the gas mask gag

Sketch of the anti-aircraft gun gone amuck

109

THE MAKING OF 1941

"See those large rubber rollers?" Logan Frazee pointed into the totally reworked Douglas house at Nicholas Beach. "The house sits on them and is held only by cables. When we snap them, the whole shooting match will roll off the cliff. We hope."

And so did every person assembled for *1941*'s grand climax. Bundled against the early morning chill were nearly every actor and crew member involved in the picture. All work on other sets had come to a momentary standstill. Nobody wanted to miss the big day—especially Steven Spielberg. He counted down the hours waiting for the fog to clear. If it didn't, he would swallow the cost of a lost production day and wait until the next morning. While everybody else chatted and drank coffee, the director paced the set and chewed his nails.

Seven cameras also waited for the sun to come out. It would be the final shot of the House scene, for, two days prior, the morning after the sub-shelling sequence had been filmed. Spielberg had made it an elaborate curtain call with almost the whole cast involved in the fade-out.

Lunchtime came and went. The crew put up a ten-dollar pool to bet on what time the shot would occur. Every quarter hour was spoken for.

A Visit to Ward's House

Going ...

Going ...

Gone!

When the clouds finally parted, the assistant directors hastily checked and double-checked all elements involved in the big shot. Most of the hundred or so observers ran to the beach for the best angle on the action. Spielberg viewed the scene from atop a hillside and communicated by walkie-talkie with the various effects men below. Flowers and Frazee operated their firing mechanisms from behind bushes near the house. Thirty cast members stood in the Douglas yard and waited for the cameras to roll.

The end came quickly. At Spielberg's radioed command, the house began to move way out over its supports. Wood splintered madly, and almost instantly the entire two-story dream house tipped over the cliff's edge. Exploding and crumbling, it slid to the crusty rocks below, where it resembled an immense woodpile.

Cheers of victory rose from the beach. The shot was a complete success. Director Spielberg spent the rest of the afternoon extending handshakes and patting backs. When it all works, the thrill is indescribable.

This time Dan Aykroyd got lucky. Earlier harassed into buying the 1:45 time slot, he had become $370 richer upon winning the pool.

Undaunted

Chapter Ten

A NEW PAINT JOB

Director Spielberg had suggested the idea of Lulubelle the tank driving through a paint factory *and* a turpentine factory in a splash of creativity. This whim eventually filled a thirty-second gap in the script and cost enough to purchase the average three-bedroom California home.

To provide for the colorful interior, they rented a vacant building with easy street access. Thirty thousand gallons of paint, donated by the Sinclair Paint Company, were rigged for the tank's wild ride. The paint was a water-base latex mixed thin to enable Lulubelle and the building to be restored to their original conditions.

Two days were spent at the paint-factory locale. It was hard to believe, but they marked the last two days of *1941*'s principal photography. Most of the scene's shooting arrangements were made in less than one week. Preparations included a raft of permits necessary to square the unusual nature of the shoot with the city. Of chief concern was the possible loss of volumes of chemical waste matter. Production manager John Wilson had a truckful of dirt standing by in case a leakage occurred in the building. A cesspool pumping outfit was contracted to vacuum the eye-popping quantity of paint that later flooded the set.

Finally, shooting commenced with the tank *exiting* through the wall of the turpentine factory. It was obviously necessary to film the "clean" portion of the sequence first. Because Lulubelle had a street curfew of twelve midnight, driver Pat Carmen was allowed little time for error. The stunt was successfully captured on film in a minimal number of takes.

For the big finale, Spielberg and Fraker placed the cameras with special care. Not an inch within the four walls could be counted on to stay dry. Spills necessitated plastic galoshes to wade through the inch-deep muck. Eventually every camera operator slipped into a raincoat as well.

High in a corner loft, A. D. Flowers and his men double-checked the effects to trigger in conjunction with the tank. Its driver walked the narrow path between the giant vats of paint. It was a challenging obstacle course: slats of two-by-fours were nailed into the concrete floor to give Lulubelle's treads something to bite into—when the gallons were set awash, the vehicle would need as much traction as it could muster. Paint was going to fly!

Stuntmen dressed as painters stood on the catwalk and paid close attention to their footing. They avoided the breakaway balsa wood sections and kept clear of the cable cutters that would drop the walkway from under them.

With everything in place, the cameras rolled and the action began. Lulubelle got off to a jack-rabbit start and the disrupted paint vats fell like rain. Arcs of color enveloped the building, creating the look of a massive finger painting. As the tank continued through the barrels, the stuntmen scrambled. Falling from the collapsed catwalk, many of them bounced and rolled off the vehicle. The maze of wreckage, coupled with the slippery floor, was very dangerous.

When Lulubelle finally came to a turf-ripping halt, it was drenched in every possible combination of primary color, resembling a war memorial painted by local schoolchildren.

One of the cameras was totally submerged in Sinclair's finest, and had to be rushed to the laboratory immediately in an effort to save the film.

When it came time for the final shot, odds ran high that it would *not* be directed by Steven Spielberg. Prone to superstition, the director had a habit of leaving before the camera made one last crank. On *Jaws,* Spielberg had

A New Paint Job

disappeared to avoid being tossed into the Atlantic by his crew. On *Close Encounters,* he had left the set in Alabama to catch an early flight back to California. But on *1941,* he broke tradition.

He directed a stuntman to slide down a section of collapsed catwalk and land squarely before the camera. Momentarily oblivious to the six inches of paint underfoot, Spielberg put his eye to the camera. The stuntman hit with a splash that sent the director stumbling backward!

Looking remarkably like a melting popsicle, Steven Spielberg bid farewell and thanks to many members of his crew. Only about half of them would participate in the final phase of the making of *1941.*

Chapter Eleven

DOG FIGHT OVER CALIFORNIA

Almost an entire month after the official end of principal photography, the *1941* camera crew returned to the Burbank studios. Assembled on Stage 15 were dozens of buildings, an entire *miniature* section of Hollywood Boulevard measuring nearly one hundred and twenty feet long.

Built for the scripted dogfight between Belushi and Matheson, the miniature was originally to consist of only five of the buildings from the real street set. And of those, only the top five floors of each would be constructed. Included were the Roosevelt Hotel, the Broadway Hollywood department store, the Security First Tower, and the Equitable Building. All were on Hollywood Boulevard in 1941. They were constructed at the same scale as Ocean Pier Park to accommodate the scale P-40 and Beechcraft models—even at one-eighth of their real size, some of the buildings stood over twelve feet high.

The set was also to have very little of the electrical lighting that had added to the great expense of the first miniature. With the city blacked out according to the script, the only frills were to be some powerful searchlight beams and perhaps some people in windows created by projectors inside the buildings.

But as Spielberg's rough cut of the movie took shape, he decided he wanted to see the entire street in more detail, right down to the pavement.

Billboards on the Hollywood Boulevard miniature

Fortunately, because of dressing the full-sized Hollywood Boulevard set earlier, all of the research necessary for the miniature replica was within reach.

The lower portions of the buildings were built on the stage during the month-long shutdown of photography. The upper portions, constructed and painted at the hangar, were then placed on top. To one side of the main group of buildings was a sloping wooden platform. To back up the foreground buildings, large cardboard boxes were painted black and arranged on the slope to form a diminishing perspective landscape of the building shapes. At the top of the incline, cutout flats representing the skyline of the Hollywood Hills were set up, complete with aluminum searchlight beams from Ocean Park and a

THE MAKING OF 1941

small but brightly lit "Hollywoodland" sign. On the set the buildings were planned to be laid out accurately, but in order to best suit the camera, they were eventually moved around.

Several weeks before shooting began, Spielberg held a meeting to finalize work on the miniature. He instructed that all building interiors were to be illuminated, and he also wanted extensive exterior lighting, lots of neon, and forty illuminated miniature Santa Clauses to exactly match the real location. The project grew overnight.

On the stage A. D. Flowers rigged both the miniature P-40 and the Beechcraft trainer on one set of guillotines running the length of the shrunken boulevard. The wires could be lowered to an inch above the Christmas string lights or raised to the building tops.

The Louma also played an important part in the second full miniature set. High above the airplane wires was a special track designed as a mount for the Louma. Hanging upside down, the camera's remote-controlled pan and tilt head was mounted on a cart that could be shuttled down the track almost as fast as the airplanes. The camera was able to chase the planes right down the center of the boulevard! As before, the camera operator could view the shot from the Louma monitor on the stage floor below. Probably the most impressive views of the miniature were the moving shots acquired by this overhead rig.

But for the entire first week of filming, the Louma track was pulled up out of the way and cameras were mounted at floor-level. A ten-second blast from the Navy fogger soaked the set in a deep smoke-haze. When cameras rolled, the planes chased one another up and down the street, narrowly missing the buildings on either side. The remarkable guillotine rig allowed them to fly upside down and do barrel rolls. For one trick shot they hurtled headlong toward each other in a game of aerial chicken. The company received an extra thrill when the two planes nearly collided at a combined speed of ninety-five miles per hour!

Dog Fight Over California

In the rush to put into working condition all of the boulevard details, numerous short-order wonders were wrought by Greg Jein's crew. Fifty quartz-halogen aircraft lamps were motorized to wave back and forth as portable searchlights. Ten expensive radio-control cars were assembled in one evening, providing scale traffic for the Hollywood streets. More than once members of the miniature crew worked all night and appeared onstage with the promised item minutes before cameras rolled.

To make the planes appear to be on fire, the effects men poured rubber cement on the wings and ignited them just before each run. Smoke charges bolted to the sides of the fuselage were also lit when the call to roll cameras came over the earphones. As soon as the burning models reached the opposite end of the set, they were doused with a fire extinguisher and the damage was assessed. Understudies for both stood ready in the wings.

In stationary shots, the waving searchlights and the airplane shadows raced across the building fronts and provided visual clues that the set was indeed huge. When the camera moved, the changing perspective made the set's colossal proportions especially evident. With the Louma flying alongside the planes, the boulevard far below looked positively awesome. The buildings at the edges of the screen blurred as they raced by at a frightening, dizzy rate. For operator Dick Colean, guiding the Louma view was almost like playing a video computer game.

One last-minute bit of ingenuity had a tremendous effect. A low-riding camera cart similar to the one used to follow the tank at Ocean Park was built: able to steer and reverse, it could motor down the street as fast as the airplanes were flying. The result was a perspective on the action that might have been taken from a speeding car.

The most complicated and the single most expensive part of the miniature was a system of movie projectors that put scale *people* into selected windows in the model buildings. To start the project, Larry Robinson chose five sophisticated 16mm projectors and engaged consultant Robin Leyden to build an electronic master-control panel for them. Synchronizing the shutters of all five projectors with the camera prevented the images in the windows from flickering.

To obtain miniature 16mm scenes for the windows, actors were filmed in simple three-wall sets built on a sound stage. For some "window views" of the street, they would walk forward and peer out as if watching the planes whiz by; for others, elaborate little skits were acted out.

By the first day of shooting, Robinson was well into perfecting the system. Spielberg counted on the figures in the windows to make the boulevard look life-size. He wanted to really "sell" the whole miniature to the audience. When the mini projectors were eventually used, actual moving figures of people could indeed be seen in the windows. The human eye could recognize that the images were only flat, two-dimensional projections, but because the camera sees monoscopically, on film the little scenes inside the windows looked as dimensional as the rest of the set!

"Sensational" was the word Spielberg used to describe the miniature on film. It looked absolutely real: the lights, the haze, the movement of searchlights and traffic, filled the screen while the airplanes zoomed overhead with convincing authority. The director was ultimately too pleased.

"We've all done our jobs too well. This miniature looks *too* real. We should blow up some of the signs and other details so the audience will know we *built* it!"

He kept his promise. The scenes did not require any appreciable damage, but for an entire day the buildings became targets for the powdermen.

In the end Spielberg spared most of the collector's item, which wasn't small enough to fit on a living-room shelf. Arrangements were made to exhibit the set on the famous Universal Studios tour.

The donation would help defray some of the project's cost, estimated at $329,000.

Chapter Twelve
WRAPPED FOR CHRISTMAS

The postproduction phase of *1941* officially began after the wrap at the paint factory. Spielberg and producer Feitshans had planned to complete the miniatures with Hollywood Boulevard and then wrap up the rest of the film with a few necessary inserts. But it was not that simple.

Some of the inserts shot in July of 1979 were of more scale models built by Jein's crew. A one-and-one-half-inch replica of the "Hollywood" sign was filmed with the P-40 Warhawk shooting down its last four letters. Then a tabletop model of the tree-trimmed La Brea tar pits, also in one-and-one-half-inch scale, was used for angles of the Beechcraft falling from the sky.

The largest and most detailed model was the Hollywood aerial miniature, a vast landscape of the Los Angeles basin. It was nicknamed the "Monopoly miniature" because its thousands of tiny buildings were no larger than the game's houses and hotels. Designed to be thirty-two by forty-eight feet in size, the model was plotted out by projecting pieces of a 1939 Los Angeles map, complete with freeways, onto 48 four-by-eight-foot platforms. It was all there—

Building a miniature Los Angeles

Sketch of the aerial view over Los Angeles

even *minuscule* representations of the Hollywood Boulevard buildings. When the entire landscape was lit up, it was transformed into a tremendous night view of half of Los Angeles.

Pickup shots were also done with John Belushi and Dan Aykroyd. Since both were committed to another movie schedule, Spielberg and a limited crew had to travel to Chicago for the shoot. Shortly after, the same crew found itself airborne in the Grand Canyon to film Wild Bill Kelso en route to the desert of California.

Consequently, with the exception of *1941*'s extravagant wrap party, the movie never formally ended. Each member of its family—and after eighteen months together, he or she knew everyone quite well—went in different directions. Many chose to take a lengthy vacation away from the rigors of motion-picture making. Others wasted no time in embarking on another film. And some were involved with *1941* until the theater prints were ready for shipping and the original negative was locked in a vault. These included film editor Michael Kahn, who worked daily with Spielberg in assembling the film; sound effects editor Fred Brown, who laid track after track of sound effects into the picture; and composer John Williams, who composed the spectacular score for *1941* and wrote individual theme music for each main character.

Wrapped for Christmas

Movie making at its best is an overwhelming experience in collaborative art. The list of those who lent their individual talents to *1941* is endless and their collective impressions of the comedy spectacular would most likely be extremely varied. But they share in common memories of miniature wonderlands, airplanes, guns, cannons, explosions, tanks, tar pits, jitterbugging, zoot-suiters, riots, explosions, Japanese sailors, air raids, pea soup, falling houses, gallons of paint, and more explosions.

For Steven Spielberg, *1941* was a personal thrill.

"Movie making is not an Olympic event—nor is it a category in the World Cup. Making films like *1941* lets life happen as I've always wanted to see it ... not as it always occurs with the dawning of each new day and the setting of the sun. It was nice to be able to manipulate reality."

When the audience responds to *1941,* whether with a stifled chuckle or a hearty belly laugh, it will be thanking every individual who participated in bringing the movie to the screen.

What next?

UNIVERSAL PICTURES AND COLUMBIA PICTURES PRESENT

CAST OF CHARACTERS

DAN AYKROYD as Sergeant Tree
NED BEATTY as Ward Douglas
JOHN BELUSHI as Wild Bill Kelso
LORRAINE GARY as Joan Douglas
MURRAY HAMILTON as Claude
CHRISTOPHER LEE as Von Kleinschmidt
TIM MATHESON as Birkhead
TOSHIRO MIFUNE as Commander Mitamura
WARREN OATES as Maddox
ROBERT STACK as General Stilwell
TREAT WILLIAMS as Sitarski
NANCY ALLEN as Donna
LUCILLE BENSEN as Gas Mama
JORDAN BRIAN as Macey
JOHN CANDY as Foley
ELISHA COOK as the Patron
EDDIE DEEZEN as Herbie
BOBBY Di CICCO as Wally

DIANNE KAY as Betty
PERRY LANG as Dennis
PATTI LuPONE as Lydia Hedberg
PENNY MARSHALL as Miss Fitzroy
J. PATRICK McNAMARA as DuBois
FRANK McRAE as Ogden Johnson Jones
STEVEN MOND as Gus
SLIM PICKENS as Hollis Wood
WENDIE JO SPERBER as Maxine
LIONEL STANDER as Scioli
DUB TAYLOR as Mr. Malcomb
IGNATIUS WOLFINGTON as Meyer Mishkin
CHRISTIAN ZIKA as Stevie

with
JOSEPH P. FLAHERTY as USO M.C.
DAVID LANDER as Joe
MICHAEL McKEAN as Willy

SUSAN BACKLINIE	Polar Bear Woman
E. HAMPTON BEAGLE	Phone Man
DEBORAH BENSON	USO Girl
DON CALFA	Telephone Operator
DAVE CAMERON	Reporter
VITO CARENZO	Vito, Shore Patrol
MARK CARLTON	Stilwell Aide
GARY CERVANTES	Zoot-Suiter
PAUL CLOUD	Stilwell Aide
LUIS CONTRERAS	Zoot-Suiter
CAROL CULVER	Anderson Sister
LUCINDA DOOLING	Lucinda
GRAY FREDERICKSON	Lt. Bressler
BRIAN FRISHMAN	USO Goon
SAM FULLER	Interceptor Commander
MARJORIE GAINES	Anderson Sister
DIAN & DENISE GALLUP	Twins
TRISH GARLAND	Anderson Sister
BARBARA GANNEN	Interceptor Assistant
BRAD GORMAN	USO Nerd
JERRY HARDIN	Map Man
DIANE HILL	Interceptor Assistant
BOB HOUSTON	Maddox's Soldier
AUDREY LANDERS	USO Girl

JOHN LANDIS	Mizerany
JOHN R. McKEE	Reporter
RONNIE McMILLAN	Winowski
DAN McNALLY	Reporter
RICHARD MILLER	Officer Miller
AKIO MITAMURA	Ashimoto
ANTOINETTE MOLINARI	Mrs. Scioli
WALTER OLKEWICZ	Hinshaw
MICKEY ROURKE	Reese
WHITNEY RYDBECK	Daffy
DONOVAN SCOTT	Kid Sailor
KERRY SHERMAN	USO Girl
HIROSHI SHIMIZU	Ito
GENO SILVA	Martinez
RITA TAGGART	Reporter
MAUREEN TEEFY	USO Girl
ANDY TENNANT	Babyface
JACK THIBEAU	Stilwell Aide
GALEN THOMPSON	Stilwell Aide
FRANK VERROCA	USO Nerd
JOHN VOLDSTAD	USO Nerd
CAROL ANN WILLIAMS	USO Girl
JENNY WILLIAMS	USO Girl
ELMER	Himself

CAST OF CREATORS

DIRECTED BY	Steven Spielberg
SCREENPLAY BY	Robert Zemeckis & Bob Gale
STORY BY	Robert Zemeckis & Bob Gale and John Milius
PRODUCED BY	Buzz Feitshans
EXECUTIVE PRODUCER	John Milius
DIRECTOR OF PHOTOGRAPHY	William A. Fraker, A.S.C.
PRODUCTION DESIGNER	Dean Edward Mitzner
EDITED BY	Michael Kahn, A.C.E.
MUSIC BY	John Williams
ASSOCIATE PRODUCER	Michael Kahn
ASSOCIATE PRODUCER	Janet Healy
EXECUTIVE IN CHARGE OF PRODUCTION	John Wilson
UNIT PRODUCTION MANAGERS	Chuck Myers
	Herb Willis
1st ASSISTANT DIRECTORS	Jerry Ziesmer
	Steve Perry
2nd ASSISTANT DIRECTOR	Chris Soldo
SPECIAL EFFECTS CREATED BY	A. D. Flowers
MINIATURE SUPERVISOR	Gregory Jein
COSTUMES BY	Deborah Nadoolman
ART DIRECTOR	William F. O'Brien
MATTE PAINTINGS BY	Matthew Yuricich
ASSISTANT FILM EDITOR	Daniel Todd Cahn
VISUAL EFFECTS SUPERVISOR	Larry Robinson
OPTICAL CONSULTANT	L. B. Abbott, A.S.C.
BLUE SCREEN CONSULTANT	Frank Van der Veer
MINIATURE LIGHTING DESIGNED BY	Robin Leyden
CASTING BY	Sally Dennison
PRODUCTION ILLUSTRATOR	George Jensen
SET DECORATION	John Austin
SET DESIGNERS	Henry Alberti
	Dan Gluck
	Greg Pickrell
	Carlton Reynolds
	Virginia L. Randolph
	William Skinner
PRODUCTION SOUND MIXER	Gene S. Cantamessa
MUSIC EDITOR	Ken Wannberg
MUSIC SCORING MIXER	John Neal
ORCHESTRA MANAGER	Marion Klein
ORCHESTRATIONS	Herbert Spencer
SUPERVISING SOUND EFFECTS EDITOR	Fred J. Brown, M.P.S.E.
SOUND EFFECTS EDITORIAL STAFF	Michele Sharp Brown, M.P.S.E.
	Alex Bamattre, M.P.S.E.
	Edward L. Sandlin
	Bub Asman
	Freddie Stafford
	Caryl Wickman
SOUND EFFECTS ASSISTANTS	Juno J. Ellis
	Lori Hollingshead
	Shelley Brown
MAKE-UP SUPERVISOR	Bob Westmoreland
HAIRSTYLES CREATED BY	Susan Germaine, C.H.D.
SCRIPT SUPERVISOR	Marie Kenney
STUNT COORDINATOR	Terry Leonard
CONSTRUCTION COORDINATOR	Mickey Woods
ADDITIONAL DIRECTOR OF PHOTOGRAPHY	Frank Stanley, A.S.C.
CAMERA OPERATION	Dick Colean
1st ASSISTANT CAMERAMEN	Ron Vargas
	Steve Bridge
2nd ASSISTANT CAMERAMAN	Richard Turner
RE-RECORDING MIXERS	Buzz Knudson
	Robert Glass
	Don MacDougall
	Chris Jenkins
ASSOCIATE TO THE PRODUCER	Mary Ellen Trainor
PRODUCTION ASSOCIATE	R. Anthony Brown
PRODUCTION COORDINATOR	Lata Ryan
SECRETARY TO MR. SPIELBERG	Gail Lyn Siemers
ASSISTANT TO MR. MILIUS	Kathleen Kennedy
PROCESS TECHNICIAN	John Russell
MATTE CONSULTANT	Jim Lyles, A.S.C.
ASSISTANT EDITORS	Darrin Martin
	Randy Morgan
ADDITIONAL 2nd ASSISTANT DIRECTORS	Bruce Solow
	Paul Moen
CASTING ASSISTANT	Stanzi Foster
CHOREOGRAPHY BY	Paul de Rolf
ASSISTANT CHOREOGRAPHER	Judy van Wormer
ADDITIONAL ILLUSTRATION	Joe Griffith
PROPERTY MASTER	Sammy Gordon
WOMEN'S WARDROBE	Mina Mittelman
ASSISTANT WOMEN'S WARDROBE	Theresa T. Volpe

MEN'S WARDROBE	Ed Wynigear
ASSISTANT MEN'S WARDROBE	Jerry Sklar
COSTUMERS	Dan North Adrienne Childers
PRODUCTION ACCOUNTANT	Margaret Mitchell
PRODUCTION ASSISTANTS	Timothy Bright Paul Martin Casella Richleigh Kerr
GAFFER	Doug Pentek
BEST BOY	Jerry Boatright
KEY GRIP	Gary Dodd
BEST BOY	John Donnelly Jack Kennedy
BOOM MAN	Raul Bruce
CABLE MAN	David Wolpa
ASSISTANT PROPERTY MASTER	Ted Mossman
PROPERTY STAFF	Lou Flemming Oscar Esquivel
ADDITIONAL SET DECORATION	Jim Hasinger
WEAPONS CONSULTANT	Syd Stembridge
DOLLY GRIP	Jan Koshay
GRIPS	Don Glenn Ty Suehiro Fredrick Albrecht Randy Vargas Bill Sutton
ELECTRICIANS	Edward J. Reilly John Wright Don Yamasaki Bill Krattiger John Cucura Tom Riffo
LEAD MAN	Tom Furginson Ray Critzas
SWING GANG	Sandy Armstrong
LOUMA CRANE TECHNICAL ADVISOR	Jean-Marie Lavalou
LOUMA CRANE OPERATOR	Andy Romanoff
2nd UNIT CAMERAMEN	Donald M. Morgan Charles W. Short
2nd UNIT ASSISTANT CAMERAMEN	Aaron Pazanti Ed Natividad
2nd UNIT GAFFER	Bill Peets
2nd UNIT KEY GRIP	Bill Beam
ASSISTANT HAIR STYLIST	Ellen Powell
ASSISTANT MAKE-UP	Jack Obringer Dottie Pearle
PUBLICIST	Saul Kahan
PUBLICITY	Pickwick Public Relations
STILL PHOTOGRAPHERS	Peter Sorel Phil Stern

CONSTRUCTION FOREMEN	Bill Wolford Joe Karras
KEY PAINTERS	Doug Wilson Edward Zingelewicz
PAINT FOREMAN	Arnold Ciaralo
SIGN WRITER	Dave Margolin
PAINTERS	Wayne Smith Ed Cornell Clyde Booten Teri Mensch D. J. Zingelewicz Glen E. Bardlerar Bernard Charron Michele Miller Hillery Clinton
TRANSPORTATION COORDINATOR	Paul Casella
TRANSPORTATION CAPTAIN	Chuck Hauer
DRIVER CO-CAPTAIN	William "Scott" Pierson
TANK OPERATOR	Pat Carmen
PILOT	Tom Camp
RESEARCH	Lillian Michaelson
OFFICE STAFF	Carol Byron Maria Melcher McConnell Davi Loren
CRAFT SERVICE	Matt Ford
MAMMAL AND VENTRILOQUIAL CREATIONS BY	Eric Von Buelow
VENTRILOQUIAL CONSULTANT	Jerry Layne
ATMOSPHERE CASTING IN ASSO- CIATION WITH HOLLYWOOD CASTING	Robert Buckingham
STUDIO TEACHER	Adria Lickliker
MINIATURE COORDINATOR	Glenn Erickson
ASSISTANT MINIATURE SUPERVISOR	Ken Swenson
MINIATURE PRODUCTION ASSISTANT	Mitch Suskin
MINIATURE PROPMAKERS	Ray Beetz Tom Cengr Michael Del Genio Anthony Doublin Ken Ebert Frances Evans David Heilman Tim Huchthausen Sharon Lee Illyanna Lowry Michael McMillen Milius Romyn Nicholas Seldon Susan Turner Gary Weeks Robert Worthington
MINIATURE RIGGING CREW	Bill Aldridge Michael Barrett Don Hathaway

Robert Johnston
David Peterson
Doyle Smiley
Richard Stutsman
Matt Sweeney
Brad Turpin

Arthur Arp
Wilbur Arp
Thomas Arp

SPECIAL
CONSULTANTS

Larry Albright
Robert Short

SPECIAL EFFECTS
TECHNICIANS

Logan Z. Frazee
Logan R. Frazee
Terry Frazee
Steve Galich
Steve Lombardi
Marlin Jones
Gary Monak
Bill Myat
Don Myers
Joe Zomar
Eugene Crum
Kenneth Estes

OPTICAL EFFECTS . Van der Veer Photo Effects
SOUND BY .... Todd-A-O
TITLES BY ...... Denis Hofman—Freeze Frame

Louma Crane courtesy of Filmtrucks Inc., New York

Film Excerpt from *Dumbo*
© 1941 Walt Disney Productions

FILMED IN PANAVISION®
PRINTS BY METROCOLOR®